"*Calm My Anxious Heart* invites us to examine a universal need for contentment. As each aspect of this need is probed, Linda gently points us to the One who can meet all the longings of our heart."

— MIMI WILSON, author of
The Once a Month Cookbook

A WOMAN'S GUIDE TO FINDING
CONTENTMENT

Calm My Anxious *Heart*

LINDA DILLOW

NAVPRESS
Discipleship Inside Out™

NAVPRESS

Discipleship Inside Out™

NavPress is the publishing ministry of The Navigators, an international Christian organization and leader in personal spiritual development. NavPress is committed to helping people grow spiritually and enjoy lives of meaning and hope through personal and group resources that are biblically rooted, culturally relevant, and highly practical.

**For a free catalog go to www.NavPress.com
or call 1.800.366.7788 in the United States or 1.800.839.4769 in Canada.**

© 1998, 2007 by Linda Dillow

ISBN-13: 978-1-60006-141-7

Cover design by studiogearbox.com
Cover image by Pierre-Auguste Renoir
Creative Team: Terry Behimer, Darla Hightower, Arvid Wallen, Kathy Guist

Unless otherwise identified, all Scripture quotations in this publication are taken from the HOLY BIBLE: NEW INTERNATIONAL VERSION® (niv®). Copyright © 1973, 1978, 1984 by International Bible Society. Used by permission of Zondervan Publishing House. All rights reserved. Other versions used include: the New American Standard Bible (nasb), © The Lockman Foundation 1960, 1962, 1963, 1968, 1971, 1972, 1973, 1975, 1977; the New Testament in Modern English (ph), J. B. Phillips Translator, © J. B. Phillips 1958, 1960, 1972, used by permission of Macmillan Publishing Company; the Living Bible (tlb), © 1971, used by permission of Tyndale House Publishers, Inc., Wheaton, IL 60189, all rights reserved; the Amplified Bible (amp), © The Lockman Foundation 1954, 1958, 1962,1964,1965,1987; the New King James Version (nkjv), © 1979, 1980, 1982, 1990, Thomas Nelson Inc., Publishers; and the King James Version (kjv).

Dillow, Linda,
        Calm my anxious heart/Linda Dillow.
        p. cm.
        ISBN 1-57683-047-0; 160006-141-9
        1. Peace of mind—Religious aspects—Christianity. 2. Dillow, Linda. I. Title.
        BV4908.5.D55 1998
248.4—dc21
                                                                98-6268
                                                                CIP

Printed in the United States of America

7 8 9 10 11 12 / 14 13 12 11 10

To the women in Eastern Europe
who lived contentment before me.

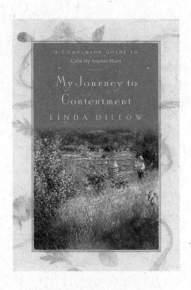

Contents

Chapter 1

My Journey to Contentment

My Journey to Contentment

As Meredith slumped into a chair in my kitchen, I prepared myself for yet another litany of her tragic life. She had asked to meet with me to talk about how she could become more content. Without a doubt, Meredith was the most negative person I'd ever met — she even looked negative!

What we are on the inside, what we continually think about, eventually shows in our words, actions, and even on our countenances. Meredith's posture and facial expression plainly revealed that she lived her own private reinterpretation of Philippians 4:8: "Finally, Meredith, whatever is untrue, whatever is not noble, whatever is not right, whatever is impure, whatever is unlovely, whatever is not admirable — if there is *anything* that is not excellent or worthy of praise — think about such things." Meredith's life was a living translation of her negative thinking.

Ironically, many women would have traded lives with Meredith in an instant. Her life was far from tragic. She was blessed with good health, a petite figure that stayed that way without effort, a husband who loved her, two adorable children, and even new furniture her husband had recently purchased to make her happy.

I asked Meredith why she was so unhappy when God had given her so many good things. Without hesitation she spouted off her complaints: First, God hadn't given her a house. She wanted her own home. She deserved it. And her husband — yes, he loved her, but she just hadn't realized his many faults. Yes, her children were adorable, but they were also negative and complaining (I didn't have to guess why!).

Meredith was like a horse with blinders on, only seeing the dirty road straight ahead. She never raised her gaze upward to God or counted her blessings. She had a blurred perspective, an unholy habit of discontent.

CONTENTMENT BEGINS WITH AN ETERNAL PERSPECTIVE

While Meredith was convinced her easy life was difficult, Ella's life was *truly* one long series of hardships. But Ella had a "holy habit" of contentment. Her vision was clear, and she lived with an eternal perspective.

What do I mean by perspective? According to Webster's, the term suggests "looking through; seeing clearly; the capacity to view things in their true relation of relative importance." I like to think of perspective as a way of seeing. An eternal perspective, then, is God's way of seeing. When we have God's perspective, we view our lives and evaluate what is important from His viewpoint. That's what Ella did.

Along with her husband and children, Ella worked as a missionary with the pygmies in Africa for fifty-two years. She had left her country, her family, and all that was familiar. Primitive doesn't begin to describe her living conditions in the scorching heat and humidity of the African bush. But Ella found no relief because electricity, air conditioning, and other modern conveniences were only a dream. Some days it was so unbearably hot that she had to bring the thermometer inside because it couldn't register past 120 degrees without breaking.

Ella's daughter, Mimi, is my friend. Mimi wondered how her mother had done it — how she had lived a life of contentment when her circumstances would have caused the hardiest to complain. Recently Mimi unearthed a treasure, a much more significant find than gold or silver. In an old diary of her mother's, she discovered Ella's prescription for contentment:

- ❧ Never allow yourself to complain about anything — not even the weather.
- ❧ Never picture yourself in any other circumstances or someplace else.
- ❧ Never compare your lot with another's.
- ❧ Never allow yourself to wish this or that had been otherwise.
- ❧ Never dwell on tomorrow — remember that [tomorrow] is God's, not ours.[1]

Her words overwhelm me; they shame me. How could Ella not complain of the weather when the perspiration dripped off her, when the stale, humid air kept her from sleeping? What made her everyday focus so different from Meredith's? The secret is in Ella's last statement. Her eyes were fixed on eternity. Her tomorrows belonged to God. She had given them to Him. And because all her tomorrows were nestled in God's strong arms, she was free to live today. One day at a time she could make the right choices and grow to possess the holy habit of contentment. Ella's focus was eternal, and her focus led to an internal contentment.

Contentment Happens on the Inside

Ella possessed *a soul sufficiency, a peace separate from her circumstances.* Most of us base our contentment on our circumstances, on our feelings, or on other people. However, true contentment is separate from our circumstances. Contentment is a state of the heart, not a state of affairs.

In *King Henry VI* Shakespeare poetically described internal contentment. A king is wandering in the country and meets two gamekeepers. He informs them that he is a king. One of them asks, "But, if thou be a king, where is thy crown?" He replies:

> My crown is in my heart, not on my head;
> Not deck'd with diamonds and Indian stones,
> Nor to be seen; my crown is call'd content
> A crown it is that seldom kings enjoy.[2]

How many women do you know who wear this crown called "content"? You can probably count them on one hand. But if I asked how many women you know who have an anxious spirit or a spirit of discontent, you would probably run out of fingers and toes counting! Contentment is rare, but it is possible.

THE SECRET OF CONTENTMENT

The apostle Paul makes an amazing statement in the book of Philippians.

> I am not saying this because I am in need, for
> I have learned to be content whatever the cir-
> cumstances. I know what it is to be in need, and
> I know what it is to have plenty. I have learned
> the secret of being content in any and every situ-
> ation, whether well fed or hungry, whether living
> in plenty or in want. I can do everything through
> him who gives me strength. (Philippians 4:11-13)

A look at Paul's life reveals how amazing these verses are. His life was full of anything but positive circumstances. He wrote them while imprisoned in a dark, dreary dungeon without sanitation, heat, or exercise equipment — elements that are a part of our American prisons. He was chained to a guard. He was lonely. I'm sure he wondered if all his work for Christ really mattered.

Paul lived an extremely difficult life. He was beaten almost to death, constantly misunderstood, deserted by friends — Paul's life was anything but perfect and controlled; yet he said, *"I have learned to be content in whatever circumstances I am."* Incredible! In other words, contentment can be *learned*. This means you and I can learn to be content.

Paul followed his extraordinary declaration about having learned to be content in all circumstances with the secret of *how* (Philippians 4:13). This often-quoted verse is translated literally from the Greek as, "I am able to face anything by the one who makes me able [to do it]." Have you ever wondered why this verse immediately follows Paul's bold statements about contentment? Paul recognized that the source and strength of all Christian contentment is God Himself.[3]

My favorite translation of Philippians 4:13 is from the late Greek scholar Kenneth Wuest.

> I am strong for all things in the One who constantly infuses strength in me.[4]

At *all* times, in all circumstances, Christ is able and willing to provide the strength we need to be content. Contentment occurs when Christ's strength is *infused* into my weak body, soul, and spirit. *To infuse* means to pour, fill, soak, or extract. Every morning when I dip my herbal tea bag into boiling water, I witness infusion.

How does God enable us to be content? He *infuses* contentment into us through His Word. As it seeps into our minds, it transforms us. Just as a cup of tea gets stronger when we give it time to steep, so we become more content when we spend time in God's Word and allow it to seep into our lives, transforming us to be like Him.

FROM CONTROL TO CONTENT

My journey to contentment began fifteen years ago when all my masterful methods of control evaporated. They quit working because life was out of control. Two of my children were on an "adolescent advance" in the wrong direction.

I had become a Christian as a college student and was excited about rearing my children in a Christian home. I had the mistaken perspective that if I pumped all the "right" things (God, His Word) into my children, they would automatically love and obey God. When it looked like my plan wasn't working, my heart was anxious and I became depressed.

When I told a friend about my fears, she observed, "Linda, you like control, and there are too many 'uncontrollables' in your life." At the time, I didn't understand what she meant. After all, I trusted God. I was a missionary — I was *paid* to trust God. What did she mean, "You like control"?

Looking back, I realize I did desire to trust God, but sometimes He was very slow. When He was moving at what I thought was a snail's pace, I unconsciously decided He needed my help. I know that sounds blasphemous. God doesn't need our help. Yet when I stepped in to massage (the truer word is *manipulate*, but *massage* sounds better!) the circumstances or to organize the people, my actions were saying, "God, You're not doing what I think needs to be done, so I'll help You out." It's our "helping God out" that leads to an anxious heart. When we take over and try to control what happens, we take our focus off the One who is in control and put our eyes on our circumstances.

Two verses guided me through those days. I memorized them, wrote them on my heart, and made a commitment to live them. First:

> God . . . is the blessed controller of all things, the
> king over all kings and the master of all masters.
> (1 Timothy 6:15, PH)

I meditated on the truths in this verse: Who controls my life? God. What kind of a controller is He? Blessed. In the words of the well-known theologian J. I. Packer, "Contentment is essentially a matter of accepting from God's hand what He sends because we know that He is good and therefore it is good."[5]

The second verse was Psalm 16:5:

> LORD, you have assigned me my portion and my cup; you have made my lot secure.

Speaker and author Elisabeth Elliot makes this thought-provoking statement about Psalm 16:5:

> I know of no greater simplifier for all of life. Whatever happens is assigned. Does the intellect balk at that? Can we say that there are things that happen to us that do not belong to our lovingly assigned "portion" ("This belongs to it, that does not")? Are some things, then, out of the control of the Almighty? Every assignment is measured and controlled for my eternal good. As I accept the given portion other options are canceled. Decisions become much easier, directions clearer, and hence my heart becomes inexpressibly quieter. *A quiet heart is content with what God gives.*[6]

Ella, the dear woman who was a missionary to Africa, knew that someone had to be "in control" of her life in this out-of-control world. Because she chose to let God be in charge instead of herself, she was a woman of contentment.

TEACUP THEOLOGY

Let's go back to our tea analogy. God has lovingly assigned each of us to be a uniquely special teacup. Perhaps we're an antique cup, painted with dainty roses set in gold. Maybe we see ourselves as an everyday cup — useful, but a little chipped around the edges. Or we could be a heavy-duty mug — rugged, unbreakable, and able to hold much.

Then God fills our cup with our portion, what He determines best. Our portion is our physical and emotional being, our abilities, circumstances, roles, and relationships.

Sometimes we don't like what's been poured into our cup. Remember the Lord Jesus in the Garden of Gethsemane? When He saw the suffering He was about to endure, He pleaded, "Father, if you are willing, take this cup from me; yet not my will, but yours be done" (Luke 22:42). Christ grasped the handle of His cup and lifted it to God and said, "I accept my portion. Infuse me with Your strength that I may drink."

Every cup — whether dainty china or rough-hewn pottery — has a handle. God has placed our portion in our cup. We either choose to grasp it by the handle and lift it to Him, saying, "I accept my portion; I accept this cup," or we choose to smash our cup to pieces, saying, "God, I refuse my portion. This cup is not the right size for me and I don't like what You've put in it. I'll control my life myself."

MY CONTENTMENT JOURNEY

Contentment is accepting God's sovereign control over all of life's circumstances. It was humbling for me to have to say to God, "I've tried to trust You, but too much of my own strength has been mixed with that trust."

The following story of two monks helped me to put my

control versus God's control into perspective.

> "I need oil," said an ancient monk, so he planted an olive sapling. "Lord," he prayed, "it needs rain that its tender roots may drink and swell. Send gentle showers." And the Lord sent gentle showers. "Lord," prayed the monk, "my tree needs sun. Send sun, I pray thee." And the sun shone, gilding the dripping clouds. "Now frost, my Lord, to brace its tissues," cried the monk. And behold, the little tree stood sparkling with frost, but at evening it died.
>
> Then the monk sought the cell of a brother monk, and told his strange experience. "I, too, planted a little tree," he said, "and see! It thrives well. But I entrust my tree to its God. He who made it knows better what it needs than a man like me. I laid no condition. I fixed not ways or means. 'Lord, send what it needs,' I prayed, 'storm or sunshine, wind, rain, or frost. Thou hast made it and Thou dost know.'"[7]

I had failed to make God my trust because I tried too hard. You may be like me or you may be at the other end of the spectrum.

You fail to make God your trust by default. Your life is out of control, so you give up. It's impossible to make sense of life, beyond impossible to be content, so you give up and give in. Most of us either try too hard or we quit trying. In both cases, we miss God. We miss His infusion of strength that leads to contentment.

This book is the story of my journey with God. How He took a first-monk woman and grew her into a second-monk woman. I am still on the journey. It is an exciting adventure! God has become my breath, my joy, my worship, my total strength. Daily He infuses His power and strength into me. He has calmed my anxious heart.

I invite you to come alongside me on the journey, to grow in your understanding of what true contentment is and how your perspective of your circumstances, yourself, your roles, and your relationships can change; to see how the barriers of anxiety, greed, and a faulty focus can keep you from possessing a heart of contentment. And, finally, I invite you to discover the bridge of trust that carries you over the barriers to contentment. Ella is not the only woman who could learn contentment. Discouraged Meredith, who thinks contentment is impossible, can learn. I can learn. You can learn, too.

And when you do learn the secret of contentment, you will see God in a new way. You will know in your heart that He is the one who is the Blessed Controller of all things, the King of kings, and the Lord of lords!

ALINA

We pushed the grocery cart around Pam Pam, my big grocery store in Vienna, Austria. Next to Safeway and Albertsons, Pam Pam left much to be desired; but compared to the small, cramped Polish stores with empty shelves, Pam Pam was a fairyland of plenty.

My companions, Alina and Henryk, were overwhelmed with the numbers and variety of goods available. When Alina picked the "just for children" toothpaste off the heavily laden shelf, I felt sick to my stomach. As we continued around the store, my nausea grew. Usually Pam Pam seemed inadequate to my American eyes, but today I saw the plenty through their Polish eyes.

Later, as we ate lunch together in my large home, I asked Alina and Henryk how they were able to accept this abundance when they knew that in two days they would return to Poland where there was no toothpaste, let alone a special toothpaste for children! I'll never forget what Alina said. "Linda, we have learned that when we are here we can enjoy the plenty, but we know that we can be just as content with little in Poland." The apostle Paul's words filled my mind. "I have learned in whatever state to be content . . . in plenty and in need."

I pushed many more carts around Pam Pam after that, but my perspective had changed. I now saw through Polish eyes, and I was humbled and blessed.

Chapter 2

———

Content
with
Circumstances

Content with Circumstances

For three years my husband, Jody, and I lived in Hong Kong, an exotic city with an unparalleled skyline, gorgeous ocean views, glitter, glamour, unbelievable wealth, and constant activity. We loved to sit at night on the edge of the bay, the salty sea breeze blowing against our faces, and look at the skyline. How I loved shopping in Hong Kong! Fa Yuen street was my haunt, my place to beat the system and unearth fabulous bargains. The raw silk suit I wore to my son's wedding cost $14, and the $150 Talbots dress I wore to my daughter Joy's wedding cost $7. Knowing her bargain-hungry mother, Joy begged me not to tell guests at her wedding how much my mother-of-the-bride dress cost. I tried, but just couldn't not tell about my incredible deal!

Grocery shopping was also a delight. I flipped on my computer and faxed the store my grocery list. The groceries, including just-caught salmon and cut-up fresh pineapple, were delivered to my doorstep that afternoon. My kind of shopping!

Travel became our middle name during our years in Hong Kong. We were privileged to visit China, Japan, South Korea, Singapore, Vietnam, and more. It was exciting to see these fascinating places and meet the unique people in each country.

In Hong Kong sunshine is a perpetual thing. We would bask in its rays on the balcony of our large hillside apartment. God graciously gave us a wonderful home, complete with hardwood floors and gloriously huge windows. Our fourth-floor view was of lush, tropical greenery and skyscrapers in the valley below.

Hong Kong's public transportation was a wonderful

alternative to fighting traffic. We didn't even own a car since the boats, buses, trains, subway, and taxis were inexpensive and omnipresent. Once a week I taught a Bible study on Lantau Island in a lovely place called Discovery Bay. To get there I walked out of my apartment, caught a bus, changed to a train, subway, jetfoil boat, and then another bus, which dropped me at the door of my Bible study destination.

My four grown children and their mates were thrilled to have the opportunity to visit Hong Kong and China. What a special time we had together! And although they lived thousands of miles away from Hong Kong, every day we could "talk" by electronic mail. What a blessing the computer age is when you live far away from those you love.

I treasured living in a city where women had an increasing hunger to know God and His Word. Because of the imminent takeover of Hong Kong by China in 1997, women were asking questions about eternal issues. My job was to train women to teach, lead small groups, and organize evangelistic coffees, so they would be prepared and in place when capitalist Hong Kong became Communist Hong Kong.

But that's only part of the story.

THE FLIP SIDE

Hong Kong *is* a fascinating place to visit, but I didn't say it was a fascinating place to *live*. Six million people reside in Hong Kong. It is one of the most densely populated places on earth. In Mei Foo, a district I visited weekly, 70,000 people live on forty acres! Living in this mass of humanity showed me how very much I like my personal space. I often felt claustrophobic there.

The shopping is great, but only at certain times because of the hordes of people. Every day is like the day before Christmas. Bargains do exist on Fa Yuen Street, but I had to search through piles of clothing to find them, and then I couldn't try anything on. I always carried a tape measure in my purse. The problem was, in order to use the measuring tape correctly I had to measure my hips — something I hadn't done in years! Not fun.

The climate is sunny, but it's also very humid. The high heat and humidity gave me heat exhaustion, and I felt listless and unwell most of the year. The walls sweat, the buildings mildew, even shoes are a breeding ground for rare fungi. Lizard-like geckos roam the walls and ceilings of every home. I never got used to having a gecko jump at me when I cleaned the bathtub. Once I squashed a baby gecko with my bare foot. I still cringe when I think about it.

The travel to exotic places was exciting but exhausting. We traveled five out of the first twelve months we lived there. I felt disoriented. I had little opportunity to adapt to a new culture or make friends.

Our apartment was wonderful, but Hong Kong has the highest rent rates in the world. After two years, our rent was raised 40 percent! I felt nauseated every month as I wrote our rent check. And each time I walked past the idol stationed outside our neighbor's door, my stomach did a flip-flop.

I never felt safe, even though we lived on the fourth floor and had five locks on our front door. One night, despite those precautions, an intruder broke into our apartment. I woke up to find the refrigerator and freezer doors open. As I looked around my kitchen, I discovered remnants of food, even a foul mixture the intruder had chewed and spit out on my stove. Obviously he didn't like our food. (How dare he!) We found evidence that someone had been in every room, including our bedroom. The prowler had stood right by my side of the bed while we slept! Violated, terrified, angry — all describe what I felt, but I was also thankful. Stories abounded in Hong Kong of people who were killed or maimed when they woke up and discovered an intruder. God kept us asleep, and I was grateful.

The public transportation is efficient but very crowded.

During peak times, pushers shove people into the subway like sardines. One morning, while I was traveling to the Bible study in Discovery Bay, a man made sexual advances toward me while we were smashed together. I jabbed my elbow in his ribs, but how do you yell "sexual abuse" when you don't speak the language and are the only non-Asian on the subway? Again I felt angry and violated. I shook all over, determined never to ride the subway again. Of course I did, but I left an hour early to miss the morning crunch.

Having our children and their spouses visit was wonderful but temporary. Across the ocean their e-mail communication was a blessing, but when my son called and said he was selling his car and moving to Bolivia, e-mail was not sufficient for me to communicate my feelings! When my daughter called and told me she was seriously ill, computer communication didn't begin to help my heart. I longed to talk to her every day, but high telephone rates prohibited long or frequent conversations.

Just as our ministry was multiplying, we began to realize that we would have to leave Hong Kong because of the Chinese takeover. After three years of learning to adapt, I had to leave, and it wasn't easy.

Life in Hong Kong doesn't sound so glamorous after all, does it?

MUD OR STARS?

Most of us can categorize our lives in both positive and negative ways. You could write a glowing list of the positives in your life, and you could then write a list of sobering negatives. Both lists are true, but the focus of each list is different.

How do you categorize your life? Take a moment right now and list the positives and negatives God has allowed in your life. If you prefer, write two paragraphs, but do write down your assessment.

Now I have a question for you, one I often ask myself: *Which list do you spend the majority of your time dwelling on?*

If you're like many women, you can relate to a young bride I heard about. Her life was not what she had hoped or expected. When she married her beloved, who was in the Marines, she thought it would be romantic and exciting to live in foreign countries and travel the globe. But two years later she was lonely and deeply discontented. She wrote a letter full of complaints to her mother. She had no friends, she couldn't speak the language and figured it wasn't worth the effort to learn since they could be moved from one country to another at a moment's notice. Worst of all, her groom was never home. She ended with "I can't take this any longer. I'm coming home."

Her astute mother faxed a reply consisting of just two lines.

> Two women looked through prison bars
> One saw mud, the other saw stars.[1]

This wise woman was telling her daughter a secret to contentment. Each of us has a choice about how we look at life: We can focus on the mud or lift our eyes and see the stars. Every woman has circumstances that appear to be prison bars. God wants you and me to learn to be content in our circumstances, not when they improve.

How is this possible?

OUR PART

In the last chapter we discussed Paul's amazing statement, "I have learned to be content whatever the circumstances." He goes on to describe two parts in the contentment process: our part and God's part. First, our part: "Do not be anxious about anything, but in everything, by prayer and petition, with thanksgiving, present your requests to God" (Philippians 4:6).

The Living Bible suggests this meaning: "Don't worry about anything; instead, pray about everything; tell God your needs and don't forget to thank him for his answers." Paul's exhortation not to worry or be anxious means that our anxiety should be used as a springboard to pray specifically. Our part in the process of learning to be content is a heart choice — a choice to pray rather than be anxious.

Paul commands us to have nothing to do with anxiety and everything to do with prayer. Sadly, many of us reverse this and worry about everything, praying only as a last resort! It's easier to worry, fret, get heartburn, lose sleep, yell at our husband or friends, the kids, or our roommates than it is to pray. We've flip-flopped the biblical prescription, not in belief but in practice.

Not only are we to pray specifically, we are to pray with thanksgiving. This is beyond difficult! When I'm worried that I have cancer or that my child is uninterested in school and failing geometry or that my friend has hurt me or that pressing problems have multiplied within me, it is hard, hard, hard to be thankful.

Psalm 116:17 helps me to understand what it means to pray with thanksgiving: "I will sacrifice a thank offering to you and call on the name of the LORD." I like this reminder because giving thanks when a black tunnel has enveloped my world is definitely sacrificial! When my little niece, Angie, fell out of a second-story window and had three skull fractures, it was a sacrificial act to pray, "Lord, You know the weight of anxiety on my heart. I can't bear being so far away when my family is in such pain. I hurt so inside, but I choose not to be anxious, and I lift little Angie to You. It's hard to find good in this situation, but I thank You, loving Father, that You love her, that she is Yours. Thank You for sparing her life. Thank You that she has access to such great medical care. I trust You to be the Blessed Controller of this terrible situation."

When confronted with negative circumstances, we have a choice: Will we pray about the problem or will we worry about it?

GOD'S PART

In Philippians 4:7 we see God's part in the contentment process: "And the peace of God, which transcends all understanding, will guard your hearts and your minds in Christ Jesus." *The Living Bible* suggests that the word *and* at the beginning of the verse means "if you do this." Do what? If we make the choice to pray instead of worry, we will personally experience God's peace. What a promise! In a world of chaos, problems, heartache, and anxiety, all of us need peace.

This verse also gives us a clue about why we don't experience peace. If you or I feel anxious and fearful instead of content, we need to ask ourselves if we've done our part. Remember, God says His peace follows our choices.

My favorite translation of this verse is "And the peace of God which transcends all our powers of thought will be a garrison to guard your hearts and minds in Christ Jesus." I visualize God encircling me with a garrison of angels whose job it is to help my poor, weak mind and heart. When anxieties multiply within me, my mind goes absolutely crazy with "what ifs." My heart, the cradle of my emotions, rocks wildly back and forth. God's peace is the exact prescription needed for my anxiety-ridden heart and mind.

What do we do if we choose to give our anxiety to God but take it back ten minutes later? I remember lying in bed many nights during one of my teenager's tumultuous years, thinking, *Did I make the right decision? How do I stop this child from heading down the path of foolishness?* I would pray through Philippians 4:6-9 but find my mind worrying again. It was as if my mind was stuck in worry mode.

I would pray, "Lord, here I am again. I was just here ten minutes ago but it didn't take; I'm still worrying instead of possessing Your peace." Again I would pray through my part and God's part in Philippians 4. Then I would start worrying again. At that point I would sit up, force my body out from under the warm covers, and go to my desk. With pen and paper in hand, I would list all the positive things the Lord had accomplished in my teenager's life in the past year. Then I'd pray over the list and thank Him that He had been at work and was still at work in her life. I'd shut off the light and go back to my cozy comforter, this time to a peaceful sleep.

THINK ABOUT SUCH THINGS

Paul comes back to our part in verse 8: "Finally, brothers, whatever is true, whatever is noble, whatever is right, whatever is pure, whatever is lovely, whatever is admirable — if anything is excellent or praiseworthy — think about such things" (Philippians 4:8).

If I had to choose my favorite verses of Scripture, Philippians 4:8 would definitely be in my top ten. These words of wisdom are framed and hanging in my living room where I am repeatedly reminded, many times each day, to dwell on the positive instead of the negative. It's hard to be in control of our minds, isn't it? Yet this is what God has asked us to do.

Proverbs 23:7 says, "As he thinketh in his heart, so is he" (KJV). The writer and philosopher Ralph Waldo Emerson put it this way: "Beware of what you dwell on for that you shall surely become." How convicting! We become what we think. Our thought life — not our circumstances — determines whether we are content. Our thought life — not our friends, husband, children, job, or *anything* else — determines our contentment!

Scripture commands us to fix our minds on the positive and also to take every thought captive (2 Corinthians 10:5). My friend Lorraine sees her thoughts being captured in this way: "My negative thoughts are like impatient toddlers jumping up and down and screaming, 'Look at me, look at me.' Jesus and I take the negative 'toddler thoughts' and send them to time-out so we can focus on the good thoughts. Sometimes they don't obey. They get up out of the chair and once again scream for attention. Then Jesus and

I take those thoughts back to the time-out chair, but this time we tie them up!"

We *must* take control of our mind. We are commanded to "be transformed by the renewing of your mind" (Romans 12:2). We renew our minds when we take negative thoughts captive and dwell on the positive.

PRACTICE MAKES PERFECT

In verse 9, Paul combined our part and God's part. "Whatever you have learned or received or heard from me, or seen in me — put it into practice. And the God of peace will be with you" (Philippians 4).

What comes to mind when you hear the word *practice?* I think of practicing the piano and learning multiplication tables as a child, and of learning German verbs as an adult. When we practice, we do something over and over. Practice isn't fun. It's boring and it's hard work. But Paul instructs us to practice "these things." What things?

- Choosing to give our anxieties to God
- Choosing to pray specifically
- Choosing to be thankful
- Choosing to dwell on the positive

We are to practice substituting prayer for worry, the positive for the negative — *and* the God of peace will be with us! For the second time in this passage we see that the peace of God follows a choice to obey. This was Paul's process, the path he walked in order to learn contentment. I have been privileged to know some dear women who have walked this path. With Paul they can say, "I have learned to be content in all circumstances."

MAKING THE CHOICE TO LOOK AT THE STARS

I met Christina when she translated for me at a marriage conference in Romania. Young, vibrant, committed to Christ, Christina
was full of dreams for her future. At the time, she was studying to
pass the university entrance exam.

Communist dictatorships, like the Romanian horror of 1981,
specialized in dashing dreams by keeping life at a survival level.
Food was scarce and heat sporadic (if available at all). Every once
in a while hot water was available, and for a few hours a day homes
had gas for cooking. It was a wonder that anyone had dreams! But
as long as the universities were open, Christina made it her goal
to attend.

She failed the exam, but not because of a low grade. She was
kept from university training because her father was a Christian
leader. How unfair! How unjust! Many would have acquired a
negative attitude, but Christina didn't. She chose to dwell on the
positive.

"Linda," she said, "I can't go to the university but I can study
and improve my English. Then I'll be a better translator the next
time you visit Romania." What a precious spirit she had! And not
just once: For seven years Christina prayed, planned, and perse-
vered in studying for the entrance exam. For seven years she was
rejected. And seven times she chose to trust that God knew what
He was doing. Yes, Christina had days of doubt, days when she
wanted to feel sorry for herself. It's never easy to choose to be content in the midst of crummy circumstances. Yet seven times she
chose to dwell on the positive.

The United States has its share of women who have learned
to be content. My friend Tammy has an incurable, degenerative
disease that prevents her from having children and will ultimately
take her life. She takes thirty pills a day for pain. I was in Tammy's
city, speaking on the topic of contentment. She got out of bed to
come to the meeting. When I asked the women to write a list of

the positives in their lives and another of the negatives, I was concerned for Tammy. Her life was filled with negatives. What positives could she write down?

When I finished speaking, Tammy came up to me and said, "Oh, Linda, it was so good for me to do that project! I had twenty things on my positive list and only four on my negative!"

In the face of such a response, I could only pray, "Oh, God, forgive me. If I lived Tammy's life, I fear my lists would be reversed."

I am still in the process of learning to be content in all circumstances. God used life in Hong Kong with its geckos, humidity, and an intruder to teach me more about surrendering to His peace.

All of us desperately need contentment, a state of inner peace separate from our circumstances. Ultimately, contentment is more a shift in attitude than a change in circumstances. Paul shifted his attitude by choosing not to be anxious and instead to pray specifically with thanksgiving. He chose to dwell on the positives, even though his life was filled with negatives. As a result, he experienced the peace of God.

All of us experience negative circumstances; some are even tragic. If that's your situation, I grieve with you in your pain. My prayer has often been, "God, don't let my pain be wasted. Use it to conform me to Your image. Use it to teach me how to be content."

When difficult circumstances come into my life, I hear God's voice saying, "Linda, let Me be the Blessed Controller. Surrender. Accept my timing. Accept my ways. Accept my outcome. Let your trust be in Me alone." His voice also says, "Linda, make secret choices that will honor Me. Though no one sees your choices or knows how difficult they are, make them for Me."

Alina, Christina, and Tammy have each made a choice about where to place their focus. You, too, have a choice. What will it be — mud or stars?

SANDA

Mentally, I retraced my plan:

Get off the train and "look Romanian."
Go to the ticket booth and put three Romanian lei on
    the counter for a tram ticket. (Pray no one asks me a
    question!)
Get on the tram going left — left, Linda, remember left.
Get off at the fifth tram stop.
Walk to the right to the third apartment complex.
Walk up to the eighth floor.
Knock on door 8B.
Stay in apartment 8B for three days while small groups
    of women come to study how they can become
    teachers of women.

*To remember this journey is to remember fear. I had never been
to this city. What if I couldn't get the ticket? What if I got lost? (My
Romanian consisted of the words for thank you, please, bread, water, and
good-bye.) I was a veteran traveler in Communist countries, but usually
I had a traveling partner. This time I was alone.*

*The plan worked like clockwork until I began the hike to apartment
8B. It was now dark outside and the stairs and landings were pitch black.
Slowly, I inched my way up each stair, counting the floors as I went.
What a relief to be on the eighth-floor landing! But still no lights. Which
door was 8B? If I knocked at the wrong door, Sanda, the hostess, could
suffer persecution, as Romanians were not to associate with Westerners.
Obviously, I couldn't pass for a Romanian with my five words. Touching
the wall as I inched toward the door, I prayed, knocked, and Sanda's dear
face appeared. Hurrah!*

Day and night, women came to this apartment for training in how to be a Bible study leader. What was so amazing about this was that Sanda's church encourages women to believe that their sole ministry is to pray for their husbands and bear children. In fact, her church teaches that a woman is saved through childbearing! (This is based on an incorrect interpretation of 1 Timothy 2:15.) Yet these women were hungry to teach others about the Bible.

Day after day, Sanda listened intently. She barely talked, and the strain of being in a group showed on her exhausted features. I couldn't help but wonder how she could lead a Bible study. Gradually, the lights turned on and she said, "I see it now. I want to give birth to spiritual children!"

What a joy to see a woman stretched, a woman willing to say, "God, I don't know my spiritual gifts. I'll try teaching, even though it scares me. I'll give mercy. I'll show hospitality. Reveal how I can be used to glorify You."

Although quaking in her boots, Sanda began leading groups in her church. After the fall of communism, she became an itinerant teacher to churches all over Romania — the expert on women's ministry in her denomination! And when her denomination hosted a women's conference, shy Sanda was one of the keynote speakers to one thousand women.

Chapter 3

———

Content
to Be Me

Content to Be Me

My daughter's voice had a new softness. "Mom, I'm pregnant! You're going to be a nana!" My thoughts immediately flew to my own nana, and to my mother, who is my children's nana. Now I was to be a nana, too. I would enter a new season of life, a new joy — a new baby!

That night I tried to sleep, but my thoughts kept returning to this new life under construction by God. I went to Psalm 139 and paraphrased it as I began to pray for my precious yet-to-be-born granddaughter:

> O God, I praise You that You are intimately acquainted with all her ways. I thank You that You have gone before her and followed her and that You placed Your hand of blessing on her head. This knowledge overwhelms me with gratitude. I thank You.
>
> Right now, You, the Master Weaver, are forming her personality and emotional makeup, weaving them together in my daughter's womb. Wonderful are Your works!
>
> You know all about my granddaughter. You are knitting together her body, soul, and spirit. As a crafter creates intricate embroidery stitches, You are superintending every detail of her beautiful design.

You have prerecorded all the days set before
her on this earth. Already You are preparing her
portion and her cup.

O God, You are great! I praise You! You have
created who she is to be but also what she is to
do. You have created her to fulfill a unique plan
ordained especially for her. Truly my grandchild is
fearfully and wonderfully made. I praise You for
Your awesome work.

Isn't it comforting to know that God knew each of us before
He created us? He planned what each of us would look like, who
our parents would be, if and who we would marry, and how many
children we would have. Before we could know God, He cared for
us. He hid each of us away as a treasure until He brought us to be.
God says that He fashioned each of us with awe and wonder.

You may be thinking, *Linda, I've read Psalm 139, I know what it says.*
If so, I want to ask you to do something for me. Would you pre-
tend you've never read it before? Open your Bible to this glorious
psalm and ask God to give you fresh eyes to see, ears to hear, and a
heart to understand what He says to you.

GOD CREATED YOUR PERSONALITY

Let's look more closely at this great psalm. It begins, "O LORD,
you have searched me and you know me" (verse 1). In other words,
every aspect of David's life was searched out and controlled by
what God knew. God was intimately acquainted with all of David's
ways (verse 3), even before He created him. Amazing! David said
God's knowledge was so complete that it was as if He had scoured
every detail of David's life. God knew David's actions, but more
incredibly, He knew his thoughts.[1]

God knows the same about you. It's difficult to comprehend,
isn't it? The Almighty Creator of the universe took personal,

intimate interest in you before your own mother knew about you.

The psalmist goes on to give examples of how intimately God knew him: "For you created my inmost being; you knit me together in my mother's womb" (verse 13). In Hebrew, "inmost being" signifies the seat of the desires and longings, the personality. Even before David was born, God shaped his personality. Likewise, when God was forming you, He created not only your body but also your emotional makeup — your personality.

David is so overwhelmed by these truths that he breaks into praise: "I praise you because I am fearfully and wonderfully made; your works are wonderful, I know that full well" (verse 14).

Have you ever thanked your Creator for His loving supervision of your creation? Have you praised Him for creating your personality? Can you say with David, "I praise you because I am fearfully and wonderfully made"? Or can you see yourself in the following description?

Carol hasn't thanked God for her personality. In fact, she feels He made a mistake when He created her. Why? Carol is an introvert and a "behind the scenes" lady. She's self-conscious about her shyness and stays away from parties and groups as much as possible. She even misses church quite often because she hates it when the pastor asks the congregation to mingle. Carol longs for her friend Sally's exuberance. Sally is always at ease in social situations.

Because Carol constantly compares her personality to those of the Sallys of this world, she has missed her own individual beauty. She has no idea why God created her; she hasn't even stopped to ask Him. She's too busy focusing on what she doesn't have instead of what God has given her.

Are you a Sally or a Carol? Why don't you stop right now and thank God for creating your distinct personality?

God Created Your Body

According to Psalm 139, God not only created your personality, He also gave you your body. Verse 15 reads, "My frame was not hidden from Thee, when I was made in secret, and skillfully wrought in the depths of the earth" (NASB).

In Hebrew, the word translated *wrought* means "embroidered." It was the same Hebrew word used to refer to the skillful and artistic needlework in the curtains of the Old Testament tabernacle. When God fashioned you in your mother's womb (described in the psalm as "the depths of the earth"), He embroidered with great skill. Although no one else could see you, God saw every detail of the formation of your body. As a weaver intricately embroiders colors together to create a beautiful pattern, God knit together your veins, muscles, nerves, and every curve and indentation that is uniquely yours. What tapestry can begin to equal the human fabric?

Perhaps you think other female tapestry is beautiful, but not yours. "I don't like my nose, my hips, my breasts. In fact I really don't like much about me." All of us could list things we'd like changed about ourselves. But if we are displeased with our physical form, we're really arguing with God. He is responsible for the color of our hair and the size of our nose and whether we have cellulite.

I'm not surprised that so many women struggle over their personal appearance. The values of our American culture are warped. We're constantly bombarded with pressure created by the media to have a "perfect" body. This emphasis is wrong and unbiblical. As Christian women, we know this perspective is twisted, yet how easy it is to get caught up in the deadly disease of comparison.

My husband, Jody, believes that women look at other women more than men look at women. This may sound strange, but I think he's right. We women analyze, scrutinize, and compare to see how we stack up to the supermodel in her skimpy bathing suit. I never come out looking very good. When we compare ourselves with others, we're told we are without understanding. *The Living Bible* says we are "stupid" (2 Corinthians 10:12).

Several years ago I read an article by the Reverend James Hufstetler that put the comparison game in perspective.

> You will never really enjoy other people, you will
> never have stable emotions, you will never lead a

life of godly contentment, you will never conquer jealousy and love others as you should until you thank God for making you the way He did.[2]

God wants each of us to praise Him for His workmanship in creating us.

George MacDonald, the man C. S. Lewis called his mentor, wrote,

> I would rather be what God chose to make me than the most glorious creature that I could think of; for to have been thought about, born in God's thought, and then made by God, is the dearest, grandest, and most precious thing in all thinking.[3]

This is a prayer of contentment.

THE CREATION OF YOUR LIFE PURPOSE

There is one final truth we can learn about ourselves from this psalm. God has a plan — a purpose — for each life: "Your eyes saw my unformed body. All the days ordained for me were written in your book before one of them came to be" (Psalm 139:16).

According to theologians, this verse has two possible meanings. One is that God divinely ordained the number of days David would live. Other Scripture suggests this interpretation as well. David said that his times were in God's hands (Psalm 31:15). Job said, "Man's days are determined; you have decreed the number of his months and have set limits he cannot exceed" (Job 14:5). The second possible meaning is that all the experiences of David's life, day by day, were written down in God's book before he was even born. In other words, God had a plan for David's life. This interpretation seems to make the most sense, considering the context of the verse.

How does this apply to us? It means that the Almighty Creator of the universe prepared a purpose for us to walk in. God acted with definite purpose when He created you because He had a plan for you to fulfill. How loved and unique you are! All of your abilities — and your disabilities — were created to fit the unique plan God has for you. No one can fulfill your purpose but you. And God's plan for you and His plan for me embrace far more than the events or circumstances that happen to us. They also embrace what God wants us to be and do and what He desires to do in and through us.[4]

In his book *Trusting God Even When It Hurts*, Jerry Bridges says that verses 13-16 of Psalm 139 must be taken as a unit.

> God created our inmost being and fashioned us in our mother's womb so that we might be equipped to fulfill the plan that He set out for us even before we were born. Who you are is not a biological accident. What you are is not a circumstantial accident. God planned both for you.[5]

According to Ephesians 2:10, you and I "are God's workmanship, created in Christ Jesus to do good works, which God prepared in advance for us to do." When I'm not pleased with the talents, gifts, and abilities God gave me, I remind myself that He is the Blessed Controller of all things (1 Timothy 6:15). If I believe this, I also must believe that God is the Blessed Controller of *my* "all things." *My* appearance. *My* personality. *My* gifts and talents. In my heart of hearts I long to please God, and it pleases Him when I am content with how He created me.

Perhaps you, too, want to be content, yet you hear the voices that say, "Be successful. Be popular. Be beautiful. Be perfect." Oh, my dear friend, stop listening to the voices. Listen to God's voice:

> Is he not your Father, your Creator, who made you and formed you? (Deuteronomy 32:6)

> Your hands shaped me and made me.... Remember that you molded me like clay.... Did you not ... clothe me with skin and flesh and knit me together with bones and sinews? (Job 10:8-11)

Helen Keller, who was both deaf and blind, wrote these thought-provoking words:

> They took away what should have been my eyes,
> (But I remembered Milton's Paradise)
> They took away what should have been my ears,
> (Beethoven came and wiped away my tears)
> They took away what should have been my tongue,
> (But I had talked with God when I was young)
> He would not let them take away my soul,
> Possessing that, I still possess the whole.[6]

This beautiful poem humbles me. Every time I read it I feel as if I should fall on my face before the Lord and ask forgiveness for whining about my insignificant disabilities. How difficult it must have been for Helen Keller to accept the physical "frame" God had given her.

So, how can we become content with the person God made us to be? Perhaps another analogy will help.

YOUR EMERGING PICTURE

The Frame. Imagine your life as a piece of art. The frame consists of your personality, your physical characteristics, and your gifts and abilities. It's probably no news to anyone that many women, instead of thanking God for the frame He's given them, spend their time trying to change it.

I once read a revealing story about such a woman. Rachel was not satisfied with the frame God built for her. She was sure her physical and emotional disabilities, her lack of abilities, were a cross she had to bear. She wished she could choose another frame.

One night as she slept, she dreamed she was led to a place where many frames lay, frames of all sizes and shapes. She discovered a beautiful frame, inlaid with jewels and gold. "Oh, this one will be perfect for me," she cried. So Rachel hung the heavy jeweled frame over her body. The gold and jewels were beautiful but far too heavy for her, and she collapsed beneath the weight of it.

Next, Rachel found a lovely frame with delicate flowers entwined around its sculpted form. This was surely the one to fit her perfectly. Hurriedly she lifted it, but beneath the flowers were piercing thorns that tore her flesh.

Wasn't there a frame just right for her? She came to a plain frame. No jewels. No delicate flowers. Yet something attracted her to it. She picked it up and hung it over her, and it proved a perfect fit. As she looked on the frame encircling her, she recognized it as the one God had originally created for her![7]

My friend, does someone else's frame look more inviting than yours? Perhaps you envy a woman whose frame is studded with jewels or decked with flowers, yet you don't know how cumbersome her frame is. Pray that God enables you to see the wisdom behind the way He framed you.

The Artwork. Now, let's consider the artwork within the frame. The art represents an emerging picture of who you are becoming. God establishes the background, then sweeps His brushstrokes across the canvas of your life in a desire to create a masterpiece. God invites you to cooperate with Him to form the picture. If you yield to His artistry, the character of Christ will be reflected through the picture of your life.

Stand back and look at the picture. What do you see reflected? Do you see the character of Christ, or do you see frantic activity? Do you try to paint with colors of character or colors of accomplishment? Too often in our lives, accomplishment and doing overshadow growth and becoming. We frantically scurry around, trying to paint the picture with our activities, but our being must be settled before our doing. George MacDonald said it well: "He thought to gain a thing by a doing, when the very thing desired was a being."[8]

What are men and women praised for in the Scriptures? For their internal character. God wants us to focus on becoming like Christ, on shaping our character into His image. This is the picture He wants to paint. We, however, tend to focus on the frame. God says our focus is distorted.

When Samuel was evaluating Jesse's sons in order to select the next king of Israel, God cautioned him, "Do not consider his appearance or his height, for I have rejected him. The LORD does not look at the things man looks at. Man looks at the outward appearance, but the LORD looks at the heart" (1 Samuel 16:7).

Unlike us, God's focus is on our inner qualities. From Solomon we learn that "a gracious woman attains honor" (Proverbs 11:16, NASB) — not a pretty woman or a clever woman, but a woman of grace. Peter emphasized this inner beauty when he described what is important to God: "Don't be concerned about the outward beauty that depends on jewelry, or beautiful clothes, or hair arrangement. Be beautiful inside, in your hearts, with the lasting charm of a gentle and quiet spirit which is so precious to God" (1 Peter 3:3-4, TLB). A woman's inward character is her adornment!

A WOMAN OF CHARACTER

A very familiar passage, Proverbs 31:10-31, gives a portrait of a woman of character and wisdom. When you read about this superwoman, what comes to your mind? A long litany of her achievements? I thought so. She was a paramount "doer." Yet, if you look carefully at the text, you will discover that all she accomplished flowed from her inner character. This woman took her knowledge of God and applied it in a skillful and successful way so that her life became a picture of beauty. It's interesting that we don't know her name or what she looked like. We don't know anything about her personality.

We do know, however, that her husband and grown children praised her. "There are many women of character but you surpass them all! Charm is deceiving, hiding an ugly personality, and beauty is only skin deep. But a woman who fears and reverences God is truly charming and lovely. Give her praise!" (verses 29-30, AMP). Did you note what they praised her for? Not because she was up at dawn, working into the night, or because she sewed their clothes, organized the home, and took food to the poor. They praised her for her spiritual character. What a tribute! Of all the women they knew, she was the best.

This exceptional woman believed that God was the Blessed Controller of her life. But she also knew that God expected her to make godly choices to rule over herself. This involved making herself attractive by the "fine linen and purple" she wore (verse 22). A more difficult choice was to rule over her tongue: "She opens her mouth with skillful and godly Wisdom, and on her tongue is the law of kindness" (verse 26, AMP). The Proverbs 31 woman was not controlled by her circumstances and the demands of her family, her household, or her home business. She was ruler of her attitudes, her time, and her schedule. Her relationship with God was central. All that she became was a result of her yielding to His sovereign control. She allowed Him to place His brushstrokes on the canvas of her life. *But* she also chose to rule her appearance, her mouth, and her activities.

FULFILLING GOD'S COMMANDS

God gives us a very interesting command in Genesis 1:28. He has just said that He created man and woman in His image, and then He gives them both a mandate: "God blessed them and said to them, 'Be fruitful and increase in number; fill the earth and subdue it. Rule over the fish of the sea and the birds of the air and over every living creature that moves on the ground.'"

Each woman is created in God's image. He has given each of us authority, responsibility, and capability. This is the real source of our identity — the source of our purpose and value. In Genesis 1:28, God gives you and me three basic commands:

- *Rule:* When we rule, we make decisions regarding a matter's course and destiny.
- *Subdue:* When we subdue, we bring something under control by conquest and maintain control by diligent maintenance.
- *Produce:* When we produce, we create value by multiplying.[9]

A domain is everything that is our responsibility. What domain has God given you? Who are the people, circumstances, and possessions in your domain? Think with me for a moment about the first important person you must rule — yourself. Each of us is to rule over our bodies, our character, and our talents. How easy it is for us to rationalize our need to obey God when it comes to controlling these areas!

Cathy constantly said that she didn't like her appearance. It wasn't God's creation she took issue with, it was the fifty extra pounds she carried. Cathy didn't have a medical problem that caused her to gain weight. She had not subdued her appetite, had not exercised her lazy body. She found it easier to complain about what God had given than to take responsibility for His gift.

Lynn's sarcasm always set people on edge. When her friends tried to confront her about her spirit, she said she couldn't help it. She said she was born with a sharp tongue and an explosive temper. It was easier to claim "heredity" than to take control and make choices to build her character.

Charlene displayed a "poor me" mentality. She claimed she had no talents. God had passed her by when He passed them out. The truth? It was more convenient to blame God than to serve Him any way she could. She didn't want to "rule and subdue her own realm." Sanda, my dear Romanian friend at the beginning of this chapter, was willing to do something that made her uncomfortable in order to discover if God could use her as a leader. Charlene, on the other hand, preferred to sit and mope.

I am convinced that a woman who struggles with her identity and purpose is a woman who has abdicated control of who she is becoming. Don't forget: God is painting a picture on the canvas of our lives. Our bodies are merely the frame. God intends to paint a beautiful picture — a picture to others of our character and unique expression of Christ's life — and place it in this frame. But He can't create this work of art without our cooperation. It needs to be a *lifelong* joint project between God and us. If you choose to criticize the frame or resist God's brushstrokes, you will not find contentment. It will elude you. If you focus on God's vision that integrates the picture with the frame, and the development of His message through you, you can say, "I am content to be me."

Leonardo da Vinci was an artist of great skill. When he was a pupil studying under his master painter, the master called Leonardo to him and asked him to finish a painting the master had begun. The man had grown old and felt the time had come to quit painting. Young da Vinci had such reverence for his master's skill that he was overwhelmed by the suggestion that he should add his strokes to the master's. The man said simply, "Do your best."

Trembling with emotion, Leonardo seized the brush and knelt before the easel to pray. "It is for the sake of my beloved master that I implore skill and power for this undertaking." As he began to paint, his hand grew steady and his eye awoke with slumbering genius. He created a masterpiece.[10]

My friend, will you take the paintbrush in your hand and kneel before your Master?

MARIANNA

My shoes sank in the thick brown mud surrounding the dreary, utilitarian apartment complex. Where were the trees and flowers? My heart pounded as several women and I crept up the seven flights of cement stairs to Marianna's one-bedroom apartment. With only four hundred square feet of living space, Marianna and her husband slept on a bed in the living room while their three children shared the bedroom.

As I entered, twenty women greeted me with hugs and kisses on both cheeks. How dear these women were! But how tired they looked. The Romanian government required that everyone — mothers included — work five and a half days a week. Food was scarce, and most women stood in line for hours before going to work each morning. That meant getting up as early as 4:00 a.m. and returning home at 6:00 p.m. The evenings were spent cooking (no mixes or McDonald's available), washing clothes (often by hand), and hanging the wash around the apartment to dry.

On top of such a strenuous physical existence, these Christians lived under an oppressive spiritual climate. Christian meetings were forbidden. If we were discovered having a Bible study, a house search, interrogation, or worse could result. Marianna had told us to begin singing "Happy Birthday" if anyone knocked on the door. Once a month the women came to these meetings; the date, time, and place passed by word of mouth or obscure phone calls such as "The birthday party will be at . . ."

I had come to this clandestine meeting to share with the women about a wife's role in marriage. Before I began, Marianna went to a cupboard and pulled out a dog-eared manuscript that said Creatora Partenera *on the cover. Through the translator, I learned this was a hand-typed copy of my book* Creative Counterpart. *Whenever a woman in the church got married, Marianna typed the bride a copy on her ancient typewriter. I was speechless.*

I remained mute as this exhausted, overworked woman talked about how she was growing in her role as a wife. "Every day when I come home from work, I take a half-hour nap. That way I can stay up longer than our eighteen-year-old son and have some time alone with my husband. We now take walks around the apartment complex so we can talk alone. I've been saving my money; in six more months I'll have enough for us to go to a hotel for a night alone together."

Her words went straight to my heart. Six months to save enough money to get a hotel room? Daily walks around a mudhole? The Lord's words echoed in my mind: "To whom much is given, much is required." How little Marianna had. How much I had been given. She chose to dwell on the positives in her role as a wife and gave all to God and to her husband. Could I say the same?

Chapter 4

Content

with My Role

Chapter 4

Content with My Role

"Linda, you are one of the few married women I know who is happy. I have observed the wives in our mission. Of the forty I know, only three are glad to be married." This sobering comment came from a single missionary woman I respected. Could she be right? Do women who love Christ and desire to serve Him truly give the impression that they are discontented in their marriages?

Fred, a singles pastor, made an equally disturbing observation. When asked if the single women in his church were content with their singleness, he replied, "Absolutely not! Every week I have weepy women in my office convinced they are doomed to a life of loneliness. They're treading water — biding time — until Mr. Right comes along. They believe that singleness is not the complete will of God."

Ironic, isn't it? Single women look at married women and wish for a husband. Married women look at their husbands and wish for different ones. Childless women long for children, and mothers long for the day when their kids will be in school.

Is it even possible to be content with your role in the here and now?

I CAN'T WAIT UNTIL . . .

Sheryl, a wife and mom; Laura, a wife, mom, and graduate student; and Terri, a single professional, are three former college roommates who keep in touch through e-mail. What follows are some excerpts from their communications that show their thoughts and struggles over the roles God has assigned them.[1] (This e-mail sketch is adapted from an original work written by Leola Floren, Michigan-based newspaper columnist and author of *The New Boss Has a Milk Mustache*.)

Dear Sheryl,

Just a quick message to let you know that Brian was named head of the chemistry department — finally! Catherine and Tim are both in high school, and the BIG news is, I'm back in school, too! I've always regretted not finishing my accounting degree, but it was too hard putting Brian through and trying to go myself. Then the kids came along ... well, you know the story ... but now it's my turn! You were so smart to finish school when you did and get that career experience under your belt before starting a family. You have it all, a successful career in your past and three darling kids in your present. Wonderwoman! Write when you have the chance.

Love, Laura

Dear Laura,

Back in school, huh? Boy, does that sound like fun! Just think. In a couple of semesters you'll be shopping for one of those expensive power suits like Elizabeth Dole wears. I'm jealous! I have a closet full of beautiful clothes, and all I wear these days are sweats. Actually, they're all I can fit into. The twins turned four last month, and I'm still trying to get rid of those last ten pounds. Yesterday I went to the supermarket with a jelly handprint plastered on my rear end. I feel like such a slob! You are sooo lucky. Gotta run. I need to get a roast into the oven, and I have car pool this afternoon.

Love, Sheryl

Dear Laura;

I flew in from Switzerland on Thursday, picked up my mail, watered some dead houseplants, and now I'm on my way to Mexico City.

Fortunately, the airline food is so bad I've lost ten pounds in the past month. Sheryl tells me you're back in school. That's wonderful! You're too bright to waste all that talent cooking pot roast and driving car pools. Thanks for trying to fix me up with that attorney on Long Island. I can't believe his name is Tony Right! Mr. Right...finally! I have the 18th through the 23rd open, and he has the 22nd through the 25th open, so we're going to try to get together for dinner on the 22nd or 23rd. More later. I need to fax some stats to a client in Geneva.

Love, Terri

Dear Terri,

Switzerland? Mexico City? I can't stand it! All I ever wanted to do was travel, but with two teens in the house, Brian and I never get to go anywhere. Catherine just got her driver's license, which is pretty scary, and Tim is so involved with sports he doesn't even want to go on vacation with us. I keep telling myself to hold on for four more years, and then I'll have all the freedom in the world. All the freedom, and no cash. Do you know what tuition is running? Even at a state school, it is outrageous. Catherine is bound and determined to go to veterinary school. I don't know why she thinks she'll like taking care of other people's pets when she won't even clean the cat box at home. You're lucky you don't have any kids to worry about.

Love, Laura

Dear Terri,

The elementary bus just picked up Adam, and the twins are down for a nap, so I might have time to finish this note. If you could see through e-mail, you'd see that my new white blouse is now purple — part of a long and complicated breakfast accident, on which I'd rather not elaborate. Suffice it to say, we now REALLY need new den carpeting. Thank you for remembering my birthday. The perfumed soap and bubble bath are a real treat, and I'm looking forward to a long soak next fall, when the twins start kindergarten. I heard from Laura a few weeks ago. She's going back to school to finish her degree. I'm so jealous! The only books I have time to read these days use the same words over and over and over: hop, pop, top, and stop. Write when you can. I know you're traveling a lot, and I like hearing about those exotic places.

Love, Sheryl

Dear Sheryl,

Wish I could spend a weekend at your house, holding Adam and the twins on my lap and reading hop, pop, top, and stop instead of these tedious sales reports. You're so lucky to have a young family that adores you. I'm still hoping, but I'm afraid my biological clock got left in another time zone. Spent last week in Paris. Overrated. I hate baguettes. Next time I have to go overseas, I'm packing a loaf of Wonderbread.

Love, Terri

Dear Laura,

Bad news yesterday. Someone from the bank called to tell me that Linda Davis was promoted to vice president. She used to report to me! She wasn't that good, either. Couldn't balance her own checkbook, and now she's on her way to the top. Terri's in Paris and complaining about the food. Can you imagine??? More later. The twins are awake and looking for grape juice. You know how dangerous that is.

Love, Sheryl

Dear Terri,

You won't believe this, but I'm pregnant! I don't know how this happened! Well, I know how it happened, I just don't understand the timing. I was looking forward to having a life of my own — finally — and now this! Why me? Why now?

Still stunned, Laura

Dear Sheryl,

Did you hear the news about Laura? The baby's due in March. She's in shock now, but I'm sure she'll warm to the idea eventually. It's almost like having a second family. Do you realize she'll be fifty-five when this kid graduates from high school? I wonder if she's thought about that? I *finally went out with Mr. Right from Long Island. What a jerk! He's way too focused on his career. He said he wants to get together again, but when I told him I was free on the 13th and the 29th, he wanted me to postpone my trip to Japan for 24 hours so we could have dinner on the 28th. Why should I be the one to juggle my schedule? Why can't I just meet a nice guy with his priorities in order who will put me first for a change? Is That Too Much To Ask?*

> *Love, Terri*

Dear Terri and Laura,

From now on I'm sending you the same e-mail message because it's all I can do to write one letter. This morning I found Adam's hamster floating in the toilet, and the day went downhill from there. The twins drank the bubble bath I got for my birthday, and the ER staff wouldn't let us go home until they both threw up. I can't wait until the kids are grown and I can go back to a nice, relaxing job with paid vacations!

> *Love, Sheryl*

P.S. When we were in school, we couldn't wait to be adults so we could do whatever we wanted. When, exactly, does that start?

Sheryl's question is a good one. When does a woman become an adult? Perhaps it's when she stops comparing her life to other women's. When she stops waiting for "Mr. Right." When she stops wishing she'd married someone else or that her children were at an easier stage.

We grow up when we see our life and our role from God's perspective; when we thank God for the role He has assigned us and begin to see our cup as a gift instead of a cross; when each morning we ask, "God, how can I glorify You today in my given role?"

WHAT ROLES DO YOU PLAY?

All of us play a role in life. A role can be defined as a "character in a play." Julia Ormond played a silly young girl infatuated with a man without character in the movie *Sabrina*. In *First Knight* she was Genevieve, a queen forced to make choices that would mean life or death for those she loved. These are two very different roles portrayed by the same actress. We use the word *role* to describe the "part" we play in life. Many of us, like Julia Ormond, play many different roles.

Elisabeth has known many roles. She was in love and desired to be married, yet she remained single for four years after she graduated from college. When she finally married her beloved, she was sure it would be forever. Two years and three months later, she had a new role: widow. For fourteen years she was single again. God surprised her with a second husband and the role of wife became hers again, this time for six years. Then once again she became a widow. She was amazed when God brought her a third husband.

Elisabeth has played all her roles gracefully because she believes each role is a gift of God. How, you ask, can widowhood or singleness be a gift? I'll let Elisabeth answer.

> At age twenty-three, God gave me the gift of singleness. At age twenty-seven, the gift of marriage. At age twenty-nine, the gift of widowhood. I was not a wife anymore. I was a widow. Another assignment. Another gift. Don't imagine for a moment that was the thought that occurred to me the instant the word of my husband's death came. "O Lord" was probably all I could think, stunned as I was.
>
> One step at a time, over the years, as I sought to plumb the mystery of suffering (which cannot be plumbed), I began to see that there is a sense in

which everything is a gift. Even my widowhood.

I say I found peace. I do not say I was not lonely. I was — terribly. I do not say that I did not grieve. I did — most sorely. But peace of the sort the world cannot give comes, not by the removal of suffering, but in another way — through acceptance.[2]

You may have guessed that Elisabeth's last name is Elliot. From her words you can see that her focus is on eternity. She is a woman who has experienced deep loneliness, a woman God has greatly used because she is wholly His.

So far in my life I've played six different roles as a mother. I've been a biological mother, an adoptive mother, a foster mother, a spiritual mother, a godmother, and a grandmother. If God pleases, someday I may be privileged to be a great-grandmother!

What roles do you play? Are you single, married, divorced, widowed? A physical mother, adoptive mother, or spiritual mother? Are you content with the roles God has given you? Do you believe that God is the Blessed Controller of your present roles? Has He given His best to you?

If we're trusting God that His portion for us is best, we can make the secret choices that will bring us a heart of contentment. If we don't accept God's portion for us, we will become women with spirits of discontent.

ALL ROLES ARE DIFFICULT

No role is without its difficulties. Perhaps your husband is not the man you thought he was or the man you hoped he would be. Perhaps your sexual relationship is not what you expected. It's hard, day in and day out, year after year, to love the same person, to seek his best. It's hard to keep marriage exciting, communication open, sex from becoming humdrum and dull. Yes, it's hard — but it's worth the effort! Jody and I just celebrated our thirty-fourth wedding anniversary, and our oneness and love are deeper with each passing year. The intimacy we experience has not come easily, but it has been hammered out in real life — day by day and year by year. I wouldn't trade what we have today for anything. Believe me, it's worth the sacrifice.

While I've never been widowed or lived as a single, my friends who have tell me that loneliness is their deepest difficulty. Elisabeth Elliot said that "in some ways all single people are misfits in society, just as someone who has lost a leg is handicapped. God meant for everybody to have two legs apiece. We don't notice them when they are both there, but if one is missing, it's noticeable." She says that as a widow she never enjoyed being a fifth wheel. "I threw things off balance simply by being there, but this was a reality I had to come to terms with."[3]

ALL ROLES PROVIDE OPPORTUNITIES

Think with me for a minute. Why did Jesus come to earth? Perhaps you can think of several reasons. Jesus gave His primary reason when He said He came not to be served but to serve, and to give His life as a ransom for many (Matthew 20:28).

He asks you and me to enter our worlds with the same purpose. Jesus humbled Himself and took the role of a servant. He used His assigned role to minister to those around Him and to give the ultimate gift of His very life. I don't think many of us have ever thought about this before, and yet if we did, I believe our attitudes would be transformed.

In his book *The Marriage Builder*, Dr. Larry Crabb says a wife will either minister to her husband or manipulate him to get her own way.[4] Which have you chosen: to minister or to manipulate?

Single women can choose to serve others as well; we don't have to be married before we can give to others.

Mothers can choose to nurture their children and cherish the time they have with them instead of waiting for the day when they're gone from home.

God has stamped "lifegiver" on all women, regardless of the role we play. Women who have no biological children may choose to ask God for the privilege of being a spiritual mother, a godmother, or a substitute mother.

If we want to be women of contentment, we must choose to accept our portion, our assigned roles from God. We must make the choice to dwell on the positive aspects of our role in life. If we don't, we'll be discontent, always wanting something different from what we've been given.

Things Could Be Much Worse

Laura, Sheryl, and Terri each made their decision. Let's read how each resolved her struggle.

Dear Terri and Sheryl,

I know I'm complaining, but life looks so hopeless. One trip to the doctor and all my plans are up in smoke. I'm too old to have a baby! Doesn't God know that? I've already put in my time at parent/teacher conferences and rainy soccer games. This isn't what was supposed to happen! I can't write more. I'm too depressed.

Love, Laura

Dear Laura,

How can you complain? All I've ever wanted is a family and a house of my own on a tree-lined street. A career isn't everything it's cracked up to be. When somebody has to go out of town on business over a weekend, who do you think they pick? Me, of course. Because no matter how much they whine and gripe about it, they don't want to miss their kids' soccer games. When I'm away for a weekend, do you think anybody cares?

Love, Terri

Dear Terri and Laura,

God tells me to be "content in all things." Oh, sure! The kids are screaming, the house is a mess, there's no milk in the fridge, and I'm wearing yesterday's underwear because I haven't had two uninterrupted minutes in the past eighteen hours! This isn't what I thought being a wife and mother would be.

Help! Sheryl

Dear Terri and Sheryl,

I'll be fifty-five when this baby graduates from high school, old enough for the senior citizen discount at Burger King! You know, maybe this isn't such a disaster. After all, if the stress doesn't kill you, kids can keep you young! Maybe there is hope!

Love, Laura

Dear Laura and Sheryl,

In my last note I was complaining about my life. But really, I do like my life most of the time. I've traveled all over the world at company expense, and I enjoy my job as much as anybody I know. I'm using my education and God-given abilities. Things could be a lot worse.

Love, Terri

Dear Terri and Laura,

My last message was full of complaining, too. Adam, Kelly, and Lynn wear me out — that's for sure! But when I'm really honest, a mother is what I want to be. When I tiptoe into their rooms late at night, I look into their small faces and think, Wow! A miracle in the making, and here I am, smack in the middle of it. That's really something.

Love, Sheryl

Laura, Terri, and Sheryl finally decided to dwell on the positive aspects of their roles. You and I can make the same choice.

WHAT DOES GOD ASK?

What is God's standard of evaluation for you and me in our given roles? Success? Perfection? His Word tells us, "Now it is required that those who have been given a trust must prove faithful" (1 Corinthians 4:2).

Faithfulness is God's standard! As His servants we are not required to be perfect or successful — simply faithful. We have been given a trust. We have been entrusted with many things: our natural gifts, our spiritual gifts, our financial resources. Our assigned role is also a trust. In His love He has given each of us the gift of singleness or the gift of marriage or the gift of widowhood. In His sovereignty, He has said it is in this role we can best glorify Him.

Will you trust Him that your assigned cup and portion come from His loving hand? Will you choose to use your role as a place to serve others? Will you pray this prayer?

> *Holy Father, You know the joys, the heartaches of my role. I confess that I have fought against what You have given. Grant me the courage to be a servant. Oh, God, I long to be faithful to You. I accept my assigned role as a gift. Teach me to "cease striving and know that You are God."*

ALINA AND LINDA

I vividly remember the day I met Alina. How could I forget my most unusual speaking experience? I remember thinking, This is a joke! These dear women can't be learning anything. I don't even know what I'm saying!

It was a wonder I could even think. The small room in the mountains of Poland was bursting with twelve women and at least twelve toddlers. Even Alina bounced her three-year-old son on her knee as she translated my words from English into Polish. Partway through the message, I remembered I had bubble gum and pencils in my purse. Strolling around the room as I spoke, I passed out gum and picked up toddlers and sat them at a table with pencils and paper. The whole scene was laughable! To my amazement, Alina thought the message was wonderful.

Later that afternoon, she took me to her home. She sat me on a stool in her kitchen and leaned down until she could look in my eyes. "Linda, teach me how to minister to women," she pleaded.

Since that day thirteen years ago, I have rejoiced to see how God used and continues to use a heart like Alina's. Thousands of women have been taught, encouraged, and counseled through Alina's words, books, and Christian magazine. And best of all, she has become my dear friend! We've never lived in the same country. Now we live oceans apart, yet the joy and "iron sharpening iron" remains. Truly, my relationship with Alina is a gift from God. All relationships are — or they should be.

Chapter 5

Content

in

Relationships

Chapter 5

Content in Relationships

I hung up the phone in shock. I thought Jana and I had a good relationship, but her irate phone call proved otherwise. How could she have said those things? If she had a problem with me, why hadn't she come to me and talked about it? I cared about Jana, about her small children. I thought I had communicated my love and care. Her scathing words hammered my heart. She had accused me of being selfish.

I tried to sleep, but her vicious words played across my mind like a tape set on automatic replay. Over and over her accusations ran through my mind. I tried to pray, to think about other things, but Jana's words had taken over my thoughts. I wanted to scream *Get out! I don't want to hear you again!* Finally I slept, only to awaken a few hours later and discover the tape was still playing.

I knew I should forgive Jana, but I felt she didn't deserve my forgiveness. I couldn't help but dwell on the injustice of her words. I prayed, I wept, I got mad at my husband, I even got mad at our dog, Barney. I knew God was displeased by my lack of forgiveness, but it was impossible to forget the words that were cemented in my heart. Betrayal hurts.

I asked twenty-five women if they had been hurt in the past year by someone they cared deeply about. Would you believe every one of them had experienced hurt or rejection of some kind? I then asked how many had intentionally or unintentionally hurt someone else. Again, everyone responded yes. The newspaper *USA Today* surveyed adults, asking them what concerns were always on their minds. The highest percentage, 64 percent, said relationships with loved ones.[1]

It's true. Much of our discontent is created as we interact and interrelate with one another. Think about your relationships. Are you 100 percent at peace with your husband? Children? Roommate? Coworkers? Family? Friends?

We're commanded in Scripture to love one another, to serve and encourage one another. When we obey these commandments, relationships bring joy and beauty to life. Nothing is so wonderful as the love of a husband, the love of a friend. And nothing is as traumatic as the betrayal of that love. I agree with my former neighbor who said, "I could be content if I just didn't have to relate to people!"

RELATIONSHIP STRUGGLES

Here are a few relationship conflicts I've heard about in the last few months.

Julie's Problem: Her Husband

"If I wasn't so angry, I'd be amused. A nosebleed threatened to tarnish the leather seats of Joel's car. I reached in the glove compartment for Kleenex and pulled out some pornographic cards. Pornography? My husband? Pornography! Those pictures! In Joel's car. Disgusting! I wanted to vomit.

"I went from a bleeding nose to a bleeding heart. How could he? I feel dirty, desecrated, defiled."

Michelle's Problem: Coworkers

"Anguish. Heartache. Rejection. Humiliation. I searched for a word to express my despair, but there was none that communicated what I felt when I was told I couldn't teach in the women's ministry program. What was most frustrating was that when I asked why, no one could give me an explanation.

"How could Christian women treat a sister like this? I had given myself for the women in my Bible study. God had used me in their lives. This was so unfair!"

Sandy's Problem: Her Roommate

"How could my best friend steal my boyfriend? Dana and I have shared a house for five years. I guess I thought neither of us would get married. But then God brought James into my life. I was convinced he was the one I had been waiting for, that this relationship would lead to marriage. Did Dana consciously try to steal him away from me? Does she have any idea how much she has hurt me? I can't continue to live in this house with her. I've lost not only my boyfriend but my best girlfriend."

Sarah's Problem: Friends

Sarah also felt betrayed. Peek into her diary:

> Oh, God, I'm scared. I'm shaking. I'm so afraid I'll die in surgery. I want to fall in love, get married, have children. God, I want to be a grandmother! I don't want to die at age thirty. My heart is racing so fast I can hear it. My hands feel clammy. My throat parched. Where are You, God? I feel so alone. Why do I have to spend the night before surgery alone in this sterile room? If only my mother weren't sick and could be here.
>
> Where are Joanie and Sue? They promised me they would come and visit me tonight — they know how afraid I am about this surgery. I

thought they understood...they promised. Where are they?

How did each of these women feel? Betrayed. I've been there. You've been there. And so has the Lord Jesus.

JESUS' EXAMPLE

All the hurt, fear, and rejection you have ever felt is what the Lord Jesus felt in the Garden of Gethsemane. When He came to the garden to pray that night, Jesus knew He was about to be betrayed and die a painful death on the cross. He had confided in His friends, telling them His heart was at the breaking point with sorrow. He had asked them to lessen His grief by staying up with Him, and they had agreed to do so. Jesus went a short distance away from them and prayed, "My Father, if it is not possible for this cup to be taken away unless I drink it, may your will be done" (Matthew 26:42). Desiring comfort, He returned to His disciples an hour later only to find them all asleep. How could three able-bodied fishermen, who had spent many sleepless nights toiling on the Sea of Galilee, be so lacking in strength that they couldn't keep awake with Him for one hour?

It's easy for us to think, *He was God in the flesh; He didn't feel hurt and rejection like I do.* But Scripture tells us Jesus was in pain. He began to be grieved and distressed. "My soul is overwhelmed with sorrow to the point of death" (Matthew 26:38). He needed His friends; He invited them to share His agony. They failed Him. And to make matters worse, this happened two more times! It's one thing to be disappointed once, but can you imagine how you'd feel if your friends continued to fail you?

You know the kind of pain friends can inflict on you. Or perhaps you're the one who has wounded and betrayed another. You were one of the friends who fell asleep when you promised to watch and pray. You were "Peter," disavowing allegiance to a friend in her time of need. The barrier in your relationship is your fault or, perhaps, both your faults. You're in a standoff, and no healing has soothed the hurt.

When we love, we open ourselves to the possibility of hurt. Much of our discontent and lack of peace comes from our expectations in our relationships. Jesus asked His friends to bear His grief with Him, and they abandoned Him. What was His response? "Rise, let us go . . ." (Matthew 26:46).

I would have cried, "Forget it! If you can't watch and pray with me while I'm sweating blood, if you can't enter into my pain after all I've done for you, if you can't forget yourselves for just one night, *forget it*! I'll walk on without you. You weren't there when I needed you. Good-bye."

Did you notice that Jesus said, "Let us go"? He used the word *us*. Even after they betrayed Him, Jesus reached out to His friends.

He forgave them, even though they had hurt Him repeatedly. He asks us to do the same. "To this you were called, because Christ suffered for you, leaving you an example, that you should follow in his steps" (1 Peter 2:21).

As I look at His response to betrayal, I am convicted. I must be willing to overlook imperfection as Jesus did. If I insist on perfection or nothing, I'll end up with nothing. I must be willing to forgive! And if you long to be content, so must you. Unless we do, our anxious hearts will not be calmed.

FORGIVENESS IS NOT AN OPTION

I will never forget the first time I visited Auschwitz, the German concentration camp in the Polish countryside. No one in our group spoke. My daughter looked like she was going to be sick. That made two of us. Auschwitz has huge glass monuments full of baby shoes, human hair, and eyeglasses, representing the thousands of people who were killed there. The walls are covered with mural-sized black-and-white photographs of World War II, many of them documenting the atrocities of the camp: the furnaces, the showers, the mass graves.

We toured the living quarters where the prisoners slept on multitiered bunk beds on mattresses of wood. When occupied, these uncomfortable sleeping quarters housed lice, fleas, and other varmints. Prisoners had a bucket to use for a toilet. Even though temperatures in Poland can drop far below freezing, the buildings had no heat. It's no wonder so few people survived.

As horrible as concentration camps were, another prison is equally torturous — the prison of bitterness. In *Growing Strong in the Seasons of Life*, Charles Swindoll poignantly expressed what happens when we're held captive by the bonds of bitterness:

> Bitterness seeps into the basement of our lives like run-off from a broken sewer pipe. Every form of ugliness begins to float to the surface of those murky waters: prejudice and profanity, suspicion and hate, cruelty and cynicism. There is no torment like the inner torment of bitterness, which is the by-product of an unforgiving spirit. It refuses to be soothed, it refuses to be healed, it refuses to forget. There is no prison more damaging than the bars of bitterness that will not let the battle end.[2]

Despite its evils, bitterness holds many of us captive. Forgiveness is the only escape route out of this prison.

But how could I forgive Jana when she had hurt me so deeply? How could Michelle forgive the women in her church? How could Sandy forgive her roommate? How could Sarah forgive her friends? And Julie — how could any woman forgive a husband who looks at pictures of naked women?

For the Christian, forgiveness is not an option. Jesus *commanded* us to forgive; He modeled forgiveness for us. Failure to forgive not only wounds our Savior but it destroys us. A lack of forgiveness causes the bitterness plant to take root in our hearts. Hebrews 12:15 says, "See to it that no one misses the grace of God and that no bitter root grows up to cause trouble and defile many."

Every mention of bitterness in the New Testament comes from the same Greek root, *pic*, which means "to cut, to prick." Peter wept bitterly after he denied the Lord (Luke 22:62). His conscience was "pricked, cut to the quick" because he had failed Jesus.

How Often Must I Forgive?

This same Peter asked the Lord: "How many times shall I forgive my brother when he sins against me? Up to seven times?" (Matthew 18:21). The rabbis said to forgive three times, so Peter thought he was being exceptionally virtuous by suggesting seven. Jesus' answer must have stopped Peter in his tracks: "I tell you, not seven times, but [seventy times seven]" (verse 22). Jesus was not suggesting 490 as the magic number of times to forgive. He was saying, "Keep on forgiving; forgive as many times as it takes." Then Jesus followed His answer with a parable about forgiveness.

> The Kingdom of Heaven can be compared to a king who decided to bring his accounts up to date. In the process, one of his debtors was brought in who owed him $10,000,000! He couldn't pay, so the king ordered him sold for the debt, also his wife and children and everything he had. But the man fell down before the king, his face in the dust, and said, "Oh, sir, be patient with me and I will pay it all." Then the king was filled with pity

for him and released him and forgave his debt.
But when the man left the king, he went to a man
who owed him $2,000 and grabbed him by the
throat and demanded instant payment.

The man fell down before him and begged
him to give him a little time. "Be patient and I
will pay it," he pled. But his creditor wouldn't wait.
He had the man arrested and jailed until the debt
would be paid in full. The man's friends went to
the king and told him what had happened. And
the king called before him the man he had forgiven and said, "You evil-hearted wretch! Here I
forgave you all that tremendous debt, just because
you asked me to — shouldn't you have mercy on
others, just as I had mercy on you?"

Then the angry king sent the man to the
torture chamber until he had paid every last
penny due. So shall my heavenly Father do to
you if you refuse to truly forgive your brothers.
(Matthew 18:23-35, TLB)

This is serious. Did you hear what Jesus said? In other words,
if I refuse to forgive Jana, my husband, my children, my colleague,
my friend, I will become a victim of torture — meaning intense
inner torment. The root of bitterness will literally eat me alive. I
will become walled in a concentration camp of my own making.

Swindoll described the consequences of an unforgiving spirit
like this: "A Christian is a candidate for confinement and unspeakable suffering until he or she fully and completely forgives others,
even when the others are in the wrong."[3]

Do you comprehend the depth of God's forgiveness toward
you? He forgave your $10 million debt. He forgave mine, too. Is
it too much for Him to ask me to forgive Jana her two thousand
dollar debt? To ask Julie to forgive her husband; Michelle, the

women in her church; Sarah, her friend; Sandy, her roommate? To ask you to forgive?

Forgiveness is the key that unlocks the door of resentment and the handcuffs of hate. Forgiveness breaks the chains of bitterness and the shackles of selfishness. While dying on the cross, Jesus said, "Forgive them" — the Roman soldiers, the religious leaders, his disciples who had fled in darkness, even you and me who have denied him so many times — "Forgive them, for they know not what they do."[4]

Author Philip Yancey called forgiveness an "unnatural act."[5] He's right. It does feel unnatural. However, forgiveness is not a feeling but a secret choice of the heart. God used my conflict with Jana to teach me this truth.

I MUST CHOOSE TO FORGIVE

A story about Clara Barton, the founder of the American Red Cross, helped me understand how I could cancel Jana's debt. One day Clara was reminded of a vicious deed that someone had done to her years before. But she acted as if she had never heard of the incident! "Don't you remember it?" her friend asked. "No," came Clara's reply, "I distinctly remember forgetting it."[6] She had made a conscious choice to forgive a vicious deed, a conscious choice to continue forgiving when reminded of the deed. By replying, "I distinctly remember forgetting it," Clara Barton was saying, "I remember choosing to forgive and I still choose to forgive."

Jana wrote to me, asking me to forgive her. After two days of inward struggle, I went before God and told Him I wanted to put down a "stake of forgiveness" as Clara Barton had done. "God, I choose to forgive Jana for the hurt she's caused me. I don't feel forgiving, but I choose in my will to forgive her." Then I went to Jana and said, "Yes, I forgive you." Did I feel forgiving? No. But I felt a sense of peace from God that I had done what was right.

I'm finding that I must *continue* to choose to forgive.

Months after I had forgiven Jana for wounding me, I discovered that several people knew about our conflict. I thought the situation was private. Here was a new knife wound to my heart. Again I went before God and said, "Lord, I choose to forgive Jana for what I knew. Now I see more harm from her actions. I choose to forgive her for this, too."

Many times the vibrations of an interpersonal conflict echo for weeks, months, even years. It's difficult enough to forgive once, but continue to forgive when the hurt just keeps on coming? And yet, this is what Jesus asks of me and of you. In fact, He asks even more.

BEYOND FORGIVENESS

I made a decision to forgive Jana and to continue forgiving her. Surely God knew how sacrificial it was for me to make this choice. I believed I was off the hook, maybe even a bit smug that I had done the godly thing. I was ready to pat myself on the back and say, "Good job, Linda, mission accomplished!" But God wanted me to go a step further. He spoke to my heart, saying, "Linda, go beyond forgiveness."

I wanted to say, "God, I've done enough!" But then I read in Romans:

> Love must be sincere. Hate what is evil; cling to what is good. Be devoted to one another in brotherly love. Honor one another above yourselves.... Bless those who persecute you; bless and do not curse.... If it is possible, as far as it depends on you, live at peace with everyone. (Romans 12:9-10,14,18)

These verses didn't say that I had to feel loving but that I was to *decide* to love, *decide* to honor. To bless is a choice of my will. I personalized these verses like this: "Linda, don't just say you love Jana, let your actions show you love her. Be devoted to Jana in sisterly love; give preference to Jana in honor. Bless Jana, do not curse her. Be of the same mind toward Jana. If possible, so far as it depends on you, be at peace with Jana."

How could I love, honor, and bless when I still didn't feel like it? Two ideas came to me as I prayed.

✣ Pray for Jana, that God will bless her.
✣ Seek to do "acts of love, acts of kindness."

As I prayed for Jana and asked, "How can I bless her?" God gave me creative ways to reach out in love. When she was discouraged about her ministry, I wrote her a letter of encouragement. When her mother visited, I invited Jana and her mother to lunch. Did I *feel* loving? No. Did I *feel* like giving a blessing? No. But God continued to prompt me to go beyond forgiveness. To put the act of forgiving into the action of forgiving. To make secret choices in my heart, in my will. My choices had nothing whatever to do with my feelings.

Going beyond forgiveness is sometimes more difficult than the initial act of forgiving. We think, *I'll forgive because God told me I had to. But I'm staying away from her from now on!* I love the picture of Jesus extending love, reaching out in a personal way to Peter after Peter denied Him, not once but three times. When the women saw the empty tomb, the angel said to them, "He has risen! . . . Go, tell his disciples and Peter, 'He is going ahead of you into Galilee. There you will see him, just as he told you'" (Mark 16:6-7).

Why did Jesus say, "and Peter"? Peter was one of the disciples; he was already included. Is it possible that Jesus knew how distraught Peter was? After swearing he had never been with Jesus, Peter needed the loving assurance that he was still one of Jesus' friends. "And Peter" was an act of love.

Is God the Blessed Controller of relationships? Yes! He allowed pain to pass into my life through Jana. He allowed Julie, Sandy, Michelle, and Sarah to feel pain. And He allows you to feel pain. The interdependent relationships in the family and in the body of Christ are some of His major tools to "grow us up." God used the betrayal of a friend to teach me to "grow up" to be more like Him.

During that time I wrote:

> I have experienced more release in my spirit in trusting God to allow me to go through any humiliation—accepting it from Him. If He thinks it is good, then I accept it. There is such a freedom in acceptance. The Word of God has been my daily delight. Not a day has passed that I have not been encouraged, challenged, comforted, or rebuked by it. I have been humbled before God. I thought I was doing well in putting a watch over my mouth. I have so much more to learn. I would walk this way again to learn what I have learned.

RELATIONSHIP CHOICES

What secret choices can you commit to in your relationships? These are mine:

- ❧ What I choose to be — faithful to God
- ❧ What I choose to do — forgive others, go beyond forgiveness
- ❧ What I choose to say — words of blessing and love

We can't control others: husband, children, friends, roommate, coworker, relatives. We can't make choices for others, only for ourselves. We can trust God, and we can control ourselves! We can do *our* part to pursue peace in relationships — and *that* brings contentment.

Catherine, a dear friend, received a letter from her estranged daughter. The letter contained family news, but between every line, this message cried out: "Please accept me, please love me, please forgive me."

Catherine had been so wounded by her daughter that she could hardly read the letter. She loved Christ, yet a bitterness had incapacitated her in her relationship with her daughter. She didn't know what to say or how to say it. So she said nothing.

Two years passed. Finally, Catherine asked a trusted friend to help her write a response to her daughter's letter. Addressed, stamped, and prayed over, the letter was mailed. It arrived one day after Catherine's death. By God's grace, Catherine was able to communicate forgiveness and love to her daughter, but not everyone is given that opportunity. Life is fleeting. God used Catherine's experience to encourage me not to wait, to forgive now.

My dear friend, do not let anything — pride, anger, not knowing how to respond or what to say — stand in the way of offering forgiveness to others.

EVA

I paced back and forth as I waited. Eva-with-No-Home was coming to my home. Our home was far from palatial, but compared to homes in Poland, it was a mansion. Many times I wanted a larger house, but today I felt guilty that God had given me so much.

Finally Eva and little Monika arrived. They would stay with us for two days and then travel to Innsbruck to visit the family Eva had lived with as a college student. As we toured our house, Eva smiled and said, "How beautiful, Linda. Everything is lovely." No greed or envy clouded her face.

I had a knot in my stomach as I mentally reviewed her housing dilemma. Because there were no apartments available for young couples in Communist Poland, Eva and her husband, Mirek, and little Monika had lived like gypsies during the three years I'd known them. First they lived with Mirek's parents, then Eva's. Back and forth from one tiny apartment to the other. Now Eva was pregnant with their second child, and the family still didn't have a home. If our situations were reversed, I'm sure my face would have been marred by envy.

After dinner Eva said she was going upstairs to wash out Monika's diapers. "Eva," I said. "You don't need to wash your daughter's diapers by hand! I have a washer and dryer. Use those." Eva replied that she was used to hand washing and it wasn't a problem.

After Monika was asleep, Eva and I sat and talked. I asked her the question that had been roaming around in my heart all day. "When you see all the modern conveniences here for mothers of small children — washing machines, disposable diapers, baby food in jars — how do you feel? Life for you in Poland is so much more difficult!"

Her response pierced my heart. "Linda, when I lived here in the West, I observed Western women. They have so many things that they don't need God."

Chapter 6

———

Never

Enough

Never Enough

We had planned to spend the summer traveling and ministering in several Eastern European countries with our children, camping in our pop-up tent camper. We stopped first in Hungary. What a revelation! I had not expected that the Dillow camping menagerie would be such a sideshow. Most Americans view a pop-up tent as the low end of the camping totem pole, but to our fellow campers, it was a Hilton on wheels. All that was available in Eastern Europe during the 1980s was one very small, very utilitarian, very much the same color, very uncomfortable style of camper.

On our first night in Hungary, we popped up our camper and I started to make dinner. Within ten minutes, thirty people were staring at us through the plastic windows. We couldn't understand what they were saying and why they were laughing and pointing at us. What were we doing that was so strange, so amusing? Since we couldn't figure out their reaction, we decided to invite them all in. So a few at a time they investigated our American marvel. Of course they went to get their friends, and we had a line of twenty people that wound around the campsite!

From there, we traveled many long hours to Romania until the crystal-clear Black Sea was before us. I wanted to be a trouper, but when I smelled the campground a half-mile before we saw it (the sewage system was inadequate), I cringed and said, "Enough, I just can't stay there." Instead we camped in a parking lot situated on a strip of land between the Black Sea and a lake. It was perfect. The sea was a two-minute stroll across the sand, and the lake (fresh water for bathing) was at our doorstep. Several families were also camped in the parking lot and, wonder of wonders, one woman was an English teacher, so we could communicate. This was definitely a plus!

We sat for hours with Carmen and her husband, talking about their life in Romania, about the little camper they had built from scraps of material, about their hopes and dreams. As I listened, I was aware that their entire focus was "more, more, more." The greatest ambition in their life was to have things, to be like those of us in the "land of plenty." When Jody and I told them about our faith in Christ and our dependence on God, they looked at us in disbelief. Why would anyone want God when they could accumulate things?

Greed is no respecter of persons. Carmen had little and was greedy, yet millionaires also suffer from the "I want" disease. John D. Rockefeller, the multimillionaire, when asked, "What else do you want most in life?" replied, "Just a little more." Regardless of whether we live in the East or the West, whether we are rich or poor, we must find contentment with what God has given.

So far we've looked at the areas in which we must learn contentment: in our circumstances, in ourselves, and in our roles and relationships. Now it's time to focus on the barriers that keep us from experiencing contentment. We will look at three barriers: greed, a lack of purpose, and anxiety.

Immanuel Kant said, "Give a man everything he wants and at that moment everything will not be everything." When a woman looks for contentment in material possessions, the "things" she wants pull her deeper and deeper into discontent. That for which she longs gradually becomes that to which she belongs.

Webster's defines greed as a "strong desire for more, especially for more than is right." Proverbs 30:15 says, "The leech has two daughters, 'Give! Give!' they cry." In other words, greed is a blood-sucking worm. Greed is insidious. Greed is disgusting. Can you visualize a leech with her two suckers crying, "Give, Give. More, More. Now, Now." Not a pretty picture, but an apt description.

God hates greed. I hate greed. Yet it is rampant. I see it all around me and I see it in me. Probably the leech lurks at your house, too. Let's look at greed in this country and in your home, then search the Scriptures for God's viewpoint and see what we can do to combat this disease.

THE STATE OF THE UNION

In his excellent book *Margin*, Dr. Richard Swenson made this statement: "At last count, there were about 210 countries in the world. Every year, Americans spend more on trash bags than the individual gross national product of 90 of these countries. Even more astoundingly, we spend more on eating out than the individual gross national product of 200 of these nations!"[1]

How did this happen? How did we acquire so much that we have more to throw away than most people own? One reason is advertising and marketing — the goal of both is to create a market for a product. What better way to do this than to persuade potential buyers they need a product?

The Sears catalog was one of the first of its kind on the market. My mother tells me that before the "Great Wish Book" arrived, people didn't know about all the things they "needed." Mother remembers feeling ecstatic because she received a doll and an orange for Christmas. But her feelings altered once she saw the Sears catalog. Night after night my mother and aunt were captivated by the unknown treasures between the catalog's covers. She tells me they began to believe they needed those treasures, they wanted those treasures, they deserved those treasures.

How times have changed! A woman I know kept track of the number of catalogs stuffed into her mailbox over a three-month period. Would you believe there were seventy? Our senses are assaulted daily. The advertising blitz is overpowering. Visual stimulation is just one of the strategies employed to help us poor consumers realize what we need. However, if we truly needed the item, the advertisers wouldn't have to work so hard at convincing us.

Need must be created, discontent stirred up. Henry Kissinger stated, "To Americans, usually tragedy is wanting something very badly and not getting it."

What a sad description.

CHARGE IT!

Not only do we want more, we aren't willing to wait for it. We want it now. As a result we buy on credit. *USA Today* revealed that Americans had $366 billion in credit card debt in 1994, up 55 percent from 1990. That's $1,400 for every man, woman, and child in the United States![2] Dave Ramsey, author of *Financial Peace: Restoring Financial Hope to You and Your Family*, believes that credit card abuse is a "culturalized disease." His statistics are frightening. The typical American carries five to seven credit cards with an average per card balance of $1,670![3]

Why are so many homes plagued by debt? Ramsey comments:

> I call it the Kellogg's kid down inside of you that likes the frosting. When it comes to finances, he or she rules: If I want something I'm going to get it, and I'm going to get it now! I tell folks, if they're ever going to get control, they have to manage that kid. The adult has to make the decisions. It's called growing up.[4]

When we're in debt, we become money's servant. The debt visible in our country as a whole and in us as individuals testifies to the fact that our "Give me! Give me!" mentality is figuratively sucking us dry.

Billy Graham has said that one of his greatest concerns for our country is its rampant greed. We have to overcome it. Greed causes a great deal of harm. When World War II was over, America was dominant. We could have been frighteningly greedy, but we turned to give help to Europe at great cost to ourselves. But over the years materialism became dominant — almost a god — in North America and Europe. Our hearts aren't satisfied by materialism. They can't be.[5]

Not only do we want what others have, our expectations continue to escalate to "more, better, and easier." Greed builds a barrier that keeps us from becoming content with what God has given.

Sadly, greed is a downward spiral that leads to envy. Envy leads to debt. All lead to discontent.

THE STATE OF THE UNION AT YOUR HOUSE

What about the state of your heart? Do you want more? Are you content with what you have or are you up to your ears in credit card debt, buying what you can't afford? It's difficult to keep perspective when we're constantly bombarded with what others tell us we "need."

The desire for more comes in different forms, some less obvious than others. I'm content with what I have until I spy what my friends call a Dillow Deal. Then greed can kick in and I overspend. During our three years in Hong Kong, I bought more than I needed because the deals were so delectable. Even though I didn't go into debt, I still was overspending. Kim is a fellow bargain junkie. Her glands salivate at the sight of a garage sale sign. You say, "Surely a garage sale is harmless." Not if it becomes an obsession, as it did with Kim. Now she must have a garage sale to sell the accumulated bargains to some other junkie.

On the other hand, Karen is a boutique junkie — no dollar

deals for her. She shopped daily at the most exclusive boutiques in town and usually returned home with bags of expensive designer treasures. When Karen met Christ, she began to see the root of her boutique hopping. "Linda, I realized that I was trying to fill needs with things."

Whether we crave inexpensive treasures or designer creations, the issue is the same: greed. When we purchase more than we can afford, we are discontent with what God has given. We no longer trust that God knows best and that He will supply our needs. How do we keep our hearts centered on God, with a thankfulness for what He has given, instead of acquiring more and more? The only way is to keep His perspective in our hearts, to burn it into our minds.

GOD'S VIEW OF "NEVER ENOUGH"

Scripture contains more references to money than to salvation. Obviously God wants us to seriously consider the issue of wealth. Sixteen of the thirty-nine parables told by Jesus deal with wealth. Scripture clearly tells us that God hates greed. But is it a sin to move from house to house, car to car, job to job to increase our possessions? What is God's perspective on abundance? Let's look at four principles found in Scripture.

1. *Everything belongs to God.* "Yours, O LORD, is the greatness and the power and the glory and the majesty and the splendor, *for everything in heaven and earth is yours.* Yours, O LORD, is the kingdom; you are exalted as head over all. *Wealth and honor come from you;* you are the ruler of all things. In your hands are strength and power to exalt and give strength to all. . . . *Everything comes from you, and we have given you only what comes from your hand*" (1 Chronicles 29:11-14, italics mine).

According to these verses, any material wealth we have is on loan to us from God. He owns it all. We do not. Therefore, the question we need to ponder is not "How much should I give?" but "How much should I keep?"

Someone might naturally say, "But I earned that money by my hard work!" In a sense this is true. But who gave us the ability to do the work? Who in His wisdom and providence made the connections that got us our jobs or saw to it that we were born in a wealthy country?

God is the Blessed Controller of *all* things. That is why James says, "Don't be deceived, my dear brothers. Every good and perfect gift is from above, coming down from the Father of the heavenly lights" (1:16-17).

2. *Heart attitude is the issue.* Psalm 62:10 says, "Though your riches increase, do not set your heart on them." God cares about where your heart is, where your treasure is. Listen to Jesus' words:

> "Do not store up for yourselves treasures on earth, where moth and rust destroy, and where thieves break in and steal. But store up for yourselves treasures in heaven, where moth and rust do not destroy, and where thieves do not break in and steal. For where your treasure is, there your heart will be also." (Matthew 6:19-21)

Jesus' words couldn't be any clearer. We are to store up treasures in heaven, not on earth where moths make holes in cloth and rust corrodes metal. Treasures deposited in heaven can never be lost.

Ask yourself: Where is my treasure? Where is my heart? Simple questions, yet the answers define who you are and what you are living for. If your treasure is on earth, your heart will be on earth also, and therefore material things will rule you.

You can quickly identify where your heart is if you will survey the things you own and then answer this question: *Suppose this trea-sure were lost, destroyed, or stolen tomorrow. Would I miss it to the point that it would harm my trust in God, my contentment, or my relationships?* If the answer is yes, then your treasure is on earth.

3. God comes first and possessions come second. "No one can serve two masters. Either he will hate the one and love the other, or he will be devoted to the one and despise the other. You cannot serve both God and Money" (Matthew 6:24).

The meaning is plain: Don't make a god out of money. Scripture never says that money or possessions are evil. You may have heard that the Bible says, "Money is the root of all evil." But this is incorrect. What it does say is, "The love of money is a root of all kinds of evil" (1 Timothy 6:10). We are told to "Keep your lives free from the love of money and be content with what you have, because God has said, 'Never will I leave you; never will I forsake you'" (Hebrews 13:5). Has your house, your dining room set, your beautiful new clothing ever said, "I will never leave you"? Why do we choose to focus on transitory things when God gives us His *guarantee* that He won't ever leave us? We cannot serve both money and God. The progression is clear: God comes first and posses-sions come second. Whom do you serve? Where is your focus?

4. Possessions are to be used, not loved. One of Jesus' most frightening warnings to contemporary America was His rebuke of the rich landowner in Luke 12. When the landowner's fields yielded a great harvest, he greedily built huge barns and stored up his earthly treasure for the years to come. *Now,* he thought, *life will be easy and secure.* God's judgment was swift. He called the landowner a fool, and that night the man's life was taken from him. "Watch out!" warned Jesus. "Be on your guard against all kinds of greed; a man's life does not consist in the abundance of his possessions" (Luke 12:15).

A. W. Tozer said it well: "Within the human heart things have taken over. God's gifts now take the place of God, and the course of nature is upset by the monstrous substitution."[6] We have mixed up what we serve and what we use. Sadly, many serve things and use God; the Scriptures instruct us to do just the opposite.

God has recently given Jody and me a wonderful gift of a house in the beautiful Colorado mountains. After eighteen years of living overseas in rented houses and apartments, I am very grateful for this gift, and yet I am also afraid. It would be so easy to let the leech get hold of me. Once something becomes mine, my human tendency is to grasp it tightly. God wants me daily to hold out my house to Him with open hands and say, "It is Yours, Lord."

I want my attitude to be like Agur, the dear man who wrote Proverbs 30. He was a humble man who saw himself in proper relationship to a Holy God. "Give me neither poverty nor riches, but give me only my daily bread. Otherwise, I may have too much and disown you and say, 'Who is the LORD?' Or I may become poor and steal, and so dishonor the name of my God" (Proverbs 30:8-9).

Agur's heart and treasure were in the right place. He served God, not things. The words of Scripture are plain: God hates greed. It's ugly. It breeds other sins. It consumes and controls us. We can't get rid of greed with a halfhearted wish or a token prayer. We must wholeheartedly come before the Lord and beg Him to remove this wretched leech with her long-reaching tentacles.

DOES GOD HAVE A STANDARD?

So far we have said four things:

- ❧ Everything belongs to God.
- ❧ Heart attitude is the issue.
- ❧ God comes first and possessions come second.
- ❧ Possessions are to be used, not loved.

Still, we haven't answered the question, What is God's standard for Christians?

As a medical doctor, Richard Swenson has the opportunity for wealth, but he and his wife have chosen to live on far less than he makes so they can give to the kingdom of God. The Swensons take literally the statement of the apostle John: "If anyone has material possessions and sees his brother in need but has no pity on him, how can the love of God be in him?" (1 John 3:17). This means the Swensons have no savings (they do have retirement and college funds). They drive used cars and seldom buy new clothes. Their lifestyle would make many Christians squirm. Is it God's standard for all Christians?

There's no simple answer to this question. God doesn't tell us specifics, but He does give us guidelines. Therefore, the question of whether we should live on $25,000, $50,000, or $200,000 a year can't be easily answered. God leads each person differently. But He won't lead us if we aren't even asking the questions.

Many people assume that as their income increases, their standard of living and their number of possessions also should increase. This may or may not be what God wants of us. We need to ask Him questions like: How much money should we give to missions and to the church?

I have asked, Should I use the extra money we received this year toward paying off our house or should I give it all away to further the kingdom of God? If I don't give all, should I give 30 percent, 40 percent, more? It's easy for me to think, *We didn't buy our home until we were fifty-three. It makes sense to put any money we have into paying off the house.* But I don't think it's that simple. God wants us to come before Him and lay down our "wealth" and say, "God, it's Yours. Show me what You want me to do with it."

WHAT CAN YOU DO AT YOUR HOUSE?

Search Your Heart

This chapter has been difficult to write because I've asked God to search me and know my heart, to test my thoughts and see if there is any wicked way in me, and I have been convicted. Of what? My lackadaisical attitude. My complacency. God's Word has burned in my heart because I long with all my being to have my treasure in heaven, to serve God and not money.

I encourage you to read Psalm 139:23-24 and pray, "God, show me where my treasure is. Help me to be honest. Show me what I can do at my house to unlatch the leech from me and my family."

You can choose to be free of the love of money. You can be in control of your possessions rather than be controlled by what you have and what you want. It's a secret choice of the heart between God and you. God can rid your heart of greed, but it's your responsibility to remove yourself from situations that promote greediness.

Cut the Ropes

Greed is like a weight attached to you by a rope. If you want to be free of greed, practice this little exercise. Stand in your house and look around. Where does greed have hold of you? Survey your possessions and ask God to show you where to cut the ropes. Maybe you need to give some clothes or other items away. This is my policy about clothes: If I don't wear it in a year, someone else needs it.

If catalogs or newspaper ad inserts cause you to covet, throw them out before reading them.

If a particular friend causes you to get the "greedies," stay away from her. Janis told me, "Every time I'm with certain friends, the discussion somehow gets around to 'my new this, my new that.' It's about what we're going to get, what we're planning and plotting to buy. It's so easy for me to get caught up in keeping up with the Joneses. All of a sudden I'm dwelling on what I don't have instead of being thankful for what I do have. I know I need to stay away from these friends."

Submit to Plastic Surgery

In the early years of our marriage, Jody and I overspent on our credit cards. We felt gut-wrenching guilt each month when the credit card bill arrived, so we took drastic action. We performed "plastic surgery," referred to by financial counselor Dave Ramsey as a "plasectomy." Out came the scissors — we cut up all of our credit cards.

Earlier I quoted Ramsey as saying that in order to get out of credit card debt, we need to grow up. Is that something you need to do? I remember the day Jody and I paid off our credit card debt. The feeling of freedom was indescribable. We still use plastic, but we're committed to paying off the bill every month.

Beware of Seasonal Greed

This last Christmas our local newspaper reported the following: "Christmas spending has tumbled so out of control that families are finding it takes into the summer and even beyond to pay off debt from gifts bought the winter before."[7]

Is this what Christ would want for His birthday celebration?

My friend Phyllis, with her husband, Paul, decided to take some steps to combat their overspending frenzy that accompanies Christmas. They began a new holiday tradition in their family. She told me: "After a Christmas of *too many* presents and a sense that we had lost the wonder of Christmas, I prayed for some new ideas for our college-age and married children. How could we communicate what was really important to us? Here's what I decided to do. Two months before Christmas, we wrote each of the children a letter, sharing that we would like their Christmas present for us to be a gift for someone less fortunate than they are. A little card on the Christmas tree would explain what they had done, in Jesus' name, for us.

"When Christmas arrived, it was such a joy to open the cards and see the creativity of the children. There were fewer wrapped presents, but so much more joy! One son sponsored an overseas orphan as his gift to us; the others washed floors and cleaned a rescue mission, and helped homeless people."

Giving a gift of yourself is appropriate anytime, not just at Christmas. Young children can also understand this concept. Why not suggest that each member of your family give a gift to the Angel Tree[8] instead of to one another? Ask God to give you creativity in your gift giving, and encourage your children to give something of themselves for Mother's Day, Father's Day, or any other time. You might suggest a coupon book of three ways they will serve you during the next year.

Brainstorm with friends about how you can say "Enough!" to overspending for gifts. Everyone's home needs a house cleaning to keep the greedy leech away.

Have an Attitude of Gratitude

We tell our children, "Don't complain," but do we practice what we preach? Elisabeth Elliot remembers that the children of the jungle tribe in South America where she ministered never complained because they had not been taught to complain. Listen to your heart. Listen to your words. Look at your actions. Are you teaching your children to be grateful for God's blessings?

Try a little experiment. For one week, make a conscious effort to be thankful. If you haven't already stored Philippians 4:8 in your memory, do it now and choose for one week to dwell on what is good, right, excellent, and praiseworthy. Ask God to develop in your heart an attitude of gratitude.

Keep a gratitude notebook and write down what happens during the week. During this experiment, determine not to ask for anything, not to gripe, grumble, or complain about what you wish you had. While you're experimenting, share with the people in your house why you're thankful for them! Thank God for your many blessings, and thank your husband and children or roommate, too. Thank your friends for their friendship. Remember, if you're upset by what you don't have, you waste what you do have.

Share Your Wealth

You may not consider yourself wealthy, but in comparison to most of the people on this planet, you're rich. (I hear you laughing!) Paul exhorts us not to be proud because we have plenty but to use our wealth to do good. Listen to his words.

> Command those who are rich in this present world not to be arrogant nor to put their hope in wealth, which is so uncertain, but to put their hope in God, who richly provides us with everything for our enjoyment. Command them to do good, to be rich in good deeds, and to be generous and willing to share. In this way they will lay up treasure for themselves as a firm foundation for the coming age, so that they may take hold of the life that is truly life. (1 Timothy 6:17-19)

We see in the Old Testament that God appointed different amounts of wealth to different servants. Daniel and Joseph were granted great wealth. Ezekiel lived in abject poverty, and Jeremiah was a "middle-income prophet." The Christian ethic teaches that wealth is a great responsibility, not that wealth is a sin. Our giving should not be like an overflow valve on our wealth, only giving the excess of a hoarded supply. Rather, it should be like a loosened

drain plug that regularly and continually lets our resources flo
others.

How are you handling the resources God has entrusted to
you? An accountant added up the percentage his Christian cli-
ents gave to Christian causes and was disturbed to discover the
average was 3 percent. Christians give $7 billion a year to churches
and Christian organizations. That sounds like a gigantic amount
until you realize that Americans spend the same amount yearly on
chewing gum. Our perspective is of utmost importance to God:
where our hope is, where our treasure is, and what we are doing
with the riches God has given us. Ten percent is only a starting
point. Why not ask God if you can give more?

BE ON THE ALERT

God has made it plain that we're to be content with what we have.
If we continue in a give-me-more mentality, we won't be content.
Happiness is getting what we want; contentment is wanting what
we get.

A story is told of Satan's agents failing in their attempts to
entice a godly woman into sin. They had tried the temptation of a
handsome man, the promise of power, and the promise of rewards.
Nothing worked. Satan told his agents, "The reason you have
failed is that your methods are too crude for one who truly seeks
God. Watch this."

Satan then approached the godly woman with great care and
whispered in her ear, "Your best friend just received a million-
dollar inheritance and bought the most beautiful house you've
ever seen." A scowl formed over her mouth and her eyes tightened
with a look of greed. Satan had won.[9]

Our best defense against Satan's traps is to be certain we're
living for eternal, not earthly, treasure. Spend a few minutes right
now to meditate on these next verses. Enter into God's presence

and pray them back to Him. Oh, that our hearts might be turned toward Him!

> ❧ I rejoice in following your statutes as one rejoices in great riches. (Psalm 119:14)
> ❧ Turn my heart toward your statutes and not toward selfish gain. Turn my eyes away from worthless things; preserve my life according to your word. (Psalm 119:36-37)

Holy Father, forgive me. I am ruled by impulses, appetites, and desires. My treasure is earthly. Change me, motivate me, and empower me by Your Spirit who indwells my weak body. I long to be content with what I have. I desire to use all You have given me for Your glory.

MRS. WONG

Mrs. Wong bowed. I bowed. Then she bowed again. How many bows are enough? I wondered, as I again smiled and bowed lower, hoping a deep bow would end this ritual.

I was privileged on this tour of China to meet some Chinese Christians. As the lone woman of the group, I had been designated the perfect one to interview Mrs. Wong. The meeting took place in a hotel room. To help Mrs. Wong feel comfortable, I had purchased some cookies from a street vendor. Fresh from the countryside, traditionally clad in a Mao suit, Mrs. Wong sat on the edge of her seat. I offered cookies once, twice, three times. My interpreter had been right — the third time was the charm! Mrs. Wong took a cookie. Niceties over, we began the interview.

"Mrs. Wong, when did you become a Christian?"

"Six years ago."

"Would you tell me about your ministry?"

"Every week I travel a ten-mile circuit on my bike. I go to six villages, one each day. On Sundays I stay home."

"Whom do you teach?"

"Five hundred to six hundred men and women."

"How did these people become Christians?"

"I told them about Jesus."

"Mrs. Wong, are you saying that in the last six years since you became a Christian you've led six hundred people to Christ?"

"Yes."

The yes was said simply, plainly, as if it was a normal, everyday occurrence to lead one hundred people to Christ every year — something anyone would do.

"Dear Lord," I prayed, "thank You for allowing me the privilege of meeting this woman of focus. Burn into my heart the conviction I see in hers."

Mrs. Wong knew why she was here. She knew what God wanted her to do with her life. She walked a path of purpose.

Chapter 7

———

A Faulty

Focus

A Faulty Focus

My nose wrinkled at the acrid smell. How very different this part of Shanghai was from the tourist areas. There was one outhouse for the residents of the entire block of apartments. Its odor assaulted me as I turned the corner, and I increased my pace to hurry past. Evidently the "honey pot men" and their wagons had not cleaned the outhouses in this part of the city for several days.

I walked past a group of elderly men playing *mahjong* under a shady tree. Several of them stared at me, and I adjusted my sunglasses to hide my round, foreign-looking blue eyes. Did I really think dark glasses would make me fit in? I'd have to dye my blond hair black, lop off a few inches of height, and definitely do something about my skin and eyes. In China, all hair is dark, all eyes are dark.

I was on my way to visit Mei Ling and her ten-year-old daughter, Ting Ting. Mei Ling was a brave woman whose purpose in life was to know Christ and to make Him known. Daily she risked her life transporting Christian materials to the underground house churches in Shanghai. As we entered her one-room apartment, I took off my sunglasses and relaxed. *Thank you, Father, for protecting me.* No one had stopped me and asked why I was in this particular district of Shanghai. Little Ting Ting stood before me and stared. She pointed to my eyes and told the translator that I had eyes like a cat. To her, I may as well have come from another planet. She ran to get her friend so she, too, could gaze at this strange woman with the light-colored eyes.

A FAULTY FOCUS

Because of my thick glasses, I was called Four Eyes in elementary school. My focus was faulty because of severe myopia, or near-sightedness. Three years ago I had radial keratotomy surgery and was given new vision. I could read the clock on the wall and see my toes in the bathtub. Amazing! My focus was corrected, and I could see clearly.

Many women today are nearsighted, not in their eyesight but in their life focus. They don't know why they're here or where they're going. They drift like a ship without a rudder. Dr. Swenson, author of *Margin*, says that aimlessness is common: "Americans are notoriously shortsighted. We live in a state of myopic mania that blurs the future. The horizon is never visible in the middle of a dust storm. But we must have a vision that extends beyond tomorrow. Living only from week to week is like a dot-to-dot life."[1]

Often women without direction live not only dot-to-dot but on hold, waiting — for the right job, the right man, a baby. Waiting for the baby to grow up and leave home — waiting for *something* to give their life meaning. Their faulty focus makes contentment an impossible dream.

Psychologist William Marston asked three thousand people, "What do you have to live for?" He was shocked to discover that 94 percent were simply enduring the present while waiting for the future.[2] Because I desire to be a woman of purpose, I often ask myself, "Linda, are you living life with a myopic focus? Are you in a waiting mode?"

Recently I read the following poem written by a fourteen-year-old boy (yes, fourteen!) who caused me to reconsider my focus.

It was spring but it was summer I wanted; the warm days
    and the great outdoors.
It was summer but it was fall I wanted; the colorful
    leaves and the cool dry air.

It was fall but it was winter I wanted; the beautiful snow
    and the joy of the holiday season.
It was now winter but it was spring I wanted; the warmth
    and the blossoming of nature.
I was a child but it was adulthood I wanted; the freedom
    and the respect.
I was twenty but it was thirty I wanted; to be mature and
    sophisticated.
I was middle-aged but it was twenty I wanted; the youth
    and the free spirit.
I was retired but it was middle-age that I wanted; the
    presence of mind without limitations.
My life was over but I never got what I wanted.[3]

SET YOUR COURSE

Imagine for a moment that you are flying to an exotic island. An
hour or so into the flight the pilot announces over the intercom,
"I have some good news and some bad news. The bad news is our
radio is out and our navigational equipment is damaged. The good
news is we have a tail wind, so wherever we're going, we'll get there
at a rate of six hundred miles an hour." While we laugh at the irony,
the sad truth is that too often we fly along like this plane — direc-
tionless but swiftly propelled by the winds of circumstances.

    Some of us walk as if in a fog when it comes to becoming women
we want to be. We spend more time planning a summer vacation
than planning our lives! If someone were to ask us where we're
headed, we'd probably answer, "Soccer practice." We get so caught
up with our kids' schedules, our car pools, our careers, our fears,
our problems that we lose sight of the bigger picture. We've forgotten who we are and that we're here for a reason. We don't stop to
think about what we do; and worse, we don't even pray about it.

That's the opposite of what God envisions for us. The Scriptures exhort us to walk wisely through this life.

> Live life, then, with a due sense of responsi-
> bility, not as [women] who do not know the
> meaning [and purpose] of life but as *those who
> do.* Make the best use of your time, despite all
> the evils of these days. Don't be vague but grasp
> firmly what you know to be the will of the Lord.
> (Ephesians 5:15-17, PH)

We must live as women who *know* the meaning and purpose of life. As Goethe, the German philosopher, put it: "Things which matter most must never be at the mercy of things which matter least." If we haven't chosen what we are living for, we're living life by default, acting out the scripts handed to us by family, other people's agendas, and the pressures of circumstances. This is *not* living as a woman who knows the meaning and purpose of life. But it's never too late to change your faulty focus.

A FIXED FOCUS

We must correct our faulty focus and become women of purpose. A good way to begin is with a purpose statement that defines what we believe and where we want to be. Many influential people throughout history have written life purpose statements. Let me share two that have had an impact on me. The first was penned by the fiery preacher Jonathan Edwards in the 1700s. I can just *feel* the strength of purpose in his words:

> Resolved, to live with all my might while I do live.
> Resolved, never to lose one moment of time, to improve
>   it in the most profitable way I can.

> Resolved, never to do anything I should despise or think
>   meanly of in another.
> Resolved, never to do anything out of revenge.
> Resolved, never to do anything that I should be afraid to
>   do if it were the last hour of my life.[4]

Jonathan Edwards wrote his life purpose statement in the form of resolutions. Betty Scott Stam wrote hers in the form of prayer:

> Lord, I give up all my own plans and purposes, all
> my own desires and hopes, and accept Thy will
> for my life. I give myself, my life, my all utterly
> to Thee to be Thine forever. Fill me and seal me
> with Thy Holy Spirit. Use me as Thou wilt, send
> me where Thou wilt, work out Thy whole will in
> my life at any cost, now and forever.[5]

Betty lived out this prayer when she and her husband became missionaries in China and were martyred after the Communists took over in 1949. This prayer of personal life purpose has been used by many people, including Elisabeth Elliot, who copied it into her Bible and signed it when she was a young girl. How that prayer must have been a reminder of what Elisabeth's life was about when, years later, her husband, Jim Elliot, was martyred by the Auca Indians, the very people they had come to serve.

I want to introduce you to four of my mature friends (mature means they qualify for the senior discount at Denny's!) and have them tell you how they live their lives with focus. Phyllis, Jean, and Mimi are grandmothers. Ney is single, but her spiritual children cover the earth. My prayer is that God will use their four stories to inspire you to fix your focus so that you can say, "This is my purpose. I know where I am going."

Phyllis

Phyllis Stanley can remember living without purpose. During college she became so disillusioned with Christianity that she closed her Bible and decided to live her own way. Two years later, she begged God to forgive her and pleaded with Him to pick up the pieces of her mixed-up life. She told God that she wanted to live the rest of her life purposefully for Him. Her life verse became Philippians 3:10: "For my determined purpose is that I may know Him that I may progressively become more deeply and intimately acquainted with Him, perceiving and recognizing and understanding the wonders of His Person more strongly and more clearly" (AMP).

Phyllis says, "When I had children, I remember thinking, *Are my children now my purpose?* I realized that my children were my *platform*, not my purpose. My purpose for life is continually in progress. I began with a verse, and years later God gave me four words that clarified my purpose." The words were: *purposely, faithfully, creatively,* and *paradoxically.*

Today, Phyllis's life purpose reads like this:

> I want to live my life very *purposely*, regularly reviewing and praying over my purpose in life, loving God intensely, cherishing and inspiring my husband, praying for and keeping connected spiritually with my children, loving women and seeking to lay spiritual foundations in their lives.
>
> I want to live *faithfully*, believing God for what I cannot see. I want to believe that God can do in my children's lives what I cannot do.
>
> I want to live *creatively*, creating beauty and warmth in my home, around my table, and in my Bible study. Creativity adds sparkle to a focused, purposeful life.

> I want to live *paradoxically*. I want to go against
> my selfish nature, against our culture, giving a
> little bit more than I feel like giving, going the
> second mile, being like Jesus.[6]

If you had the privilege to know Phyllis, you would clearly see these four words reflected in her life.

Jean

Jean Fleming is a deep thinker and a woman who lives a focused life. When I asked Jean how she would define her purpose statement, she replied, "I want to influence generations." Psalm 78:1-5 records Jean's desire to pass on the deep truth of God to her children and grandchildren. "Tell the next generation the praiseworthy deeds of the LORD, his power, and the wonders he has done" (Psalm 78:4).

It's difficult to live a focused life with the hope of leaving a legacy to future generations. Jean stated in her excellent book *Finding Focus in a Whirlwind World*, "As we seek to focus life, a formidable problem becomes apparent. Life loses focus without any effort, determination, or decision on our part. The process of living, day in and day out, tends to dilute and divert focus. We become so busy that we have no time to consider *how* we live. Plato said the unexamined life is a life not worth living."[7]

To maintain focus in the grind of daily living, Jean pictures her life as a tree. The trunk represents her relationship to Christ; the limbs represent major areas of God-given responsibility, such as family, job, ministry, and personal development. The branches of Jean's tree are the activities and opportunities of life. Sometimes the "activity branches" mushroom and multiply, obscuring the trunk and limbs. When this happens, Jean says she feels trapped, frustrated, and empty. "I must go beyond defining life by activities. I must focus not on the branches, but on the trunk and limbs.

...at I do because of Jesus and His claim on my life. I don't do what I don't do for the same reason."

For Jean, living with focus means she has to prune her tree. "Three or four times a year I spend half a day with the Lord to evaluate my life, to examine my schedule, and to set new direction for the months ahead. I spend most of the time reading the Bible, praying, and singing to the Lord. This quiet time acts like a knife to cut through the illusions and mirages of everyday life. It enables me to focus my attention, to set my heart on things above."

During her retreat, Jean lays out her "tree" before the Lord and asks, "Lord, at this point in my life, what must I do to keep my relationship to You vital? To what do You want me to say yes and to what do You want me to say no?"

Does Jean always have a clear direction of what she should do after her half day of pruning? No. But she told me that as she listens for His voice, spiritually straining to hear what He wants to say, her heart is brought into alignment with God.[8]

Jean's godly focus is a direct result of her decision to prune her tree and commune with her God.

Ney

Ney Bailey's life purpose statement is made up of two Scripture passages and a prayer. At age twenty-four, she set her life goal around Romans 8:28-29: "And we know that God causes all things to work together for good to those who love God, to those who are called according to His purpose. For whom He foreknew, He also predestined *to become conformed to the image of His Son*" (NASB, italics mine).

As Ney fixed her focus to become conformed to Christ, she personally applied these verses to specific situations in her life. "When things happened that I didn't like, I thanked Him, even though I didn't understand. I knew the negative circumstances were part of His conforming me."

Ten years later, God impressed a second passage of Scripture on Ney's heart. She knelt before an altar and committed herself to live Isaiah 61:1-3 (NASB).

> The Spirit of the Lord GOD is upon me, because the LORD has anointed me to bring good news to the afflicted; He has sent me to bind up the brokenhearted, to proclaim liberty to captives, and freedom to prisoners; to proclaim the favorable year of the Lord, and the day of vengeance of our GOD; to comfort all who mourn, to grant those who mourn in Zion, giving them a garland instead of ashes, the oil of gladness instead of mourning, the mantle of praise instead of a spirit of fainting. So they will be called oaks of righteousness, the planting of the LORD, that He may be glorified.

As Ney's friend, I marvel at how specifically her life exemplifies these verses. She *does* bring good news to the afflicted, bind up the brokenhearted, and proclaim liberty to captives and freedom to prisoners. She *does* give the oil of gladness instead of mourning, the mantle of praise instead of a spirit of fainting.[9]

Twenty years later, Ney heard the following prayer and claimed it as her own:

> Lord Jesus, I offer You
> All that I am
> All that I have
> All that I do
> All that I suffer
> Now and Forever.[10]

To personalize this beautiful prayer, Ney took four pieces of paper and labeled them: (1) All that I am, (2) All that I have,

(3) All that I do, and (4) All that I suffer. "I wrote out everything I could think of that belonged in the four categories." She says, "I knew that whatever was listed on my four pages was material for sacrifice. So after making my lists, I thanked God for those things and surrendered them to Him as an offering."

Ney's purpose statement has progressed over the years, and God's work of conforming her to His image is beautifully apparent to all who know her.

Mimi

When Mimi Wilson was thirty, she began to wonder how the women she admired became women of excellence. She wanted to understand so she could pattern her life after them. She says, "I read books, observed and studied women, and asked lots of questions. God gave me a desire for a focused purpose. It was as if He pulled me into a room called *understanding*. In that room, I meditated on questions like, Why am I here? Where am I going? What is my purpose in life? When I reached this first room, I realized that a second room called *decision* lay beyond it. Answering the questions wasn't enough; the first room was merely a stepping-stone. I now had to act upon what I discovered in the room of understanding. That involved making decisions.

"By the time I was thirty-two, I saw my life in view of eternity. I realized eternity did not begin when I died. My eternity had already begun! So I pictured my life as an eternal line. I stood on the left edge of the line and looked toward the end of my life on the right.

Mimi 32 ——————————————————— 80

"Two important questions came to my mind: First, what did I want to be at age eighty? That was the easy part. I knew the answer.

❧ A woman of contentment
❧ A woman of wisdom
❧ A woman of godliness

"The second question — which took longer to answer — was, How was I going to become that woman? I knew it began with a deeper knowledge of God's character."

Beginning at age thirty-two, Mimi spent one morning a week in prayer, dwelling on the character of God. If you have ever tried to pray with three small children circled around your knees, you realize this was very difficult to arrange. How did Mimi do it? "I didn't want the children to hate my God because He had my attention during my prayer times. So before I prayed, I gave my three cherubs big portions of "cream" (concentrated time with Mommy and special treats). Was it worth the effort? I would have moved heaven and earth to have the intimate time with the Lord because He met me and showed me Himself. When I left the times of prayer, I had a new view of eternity, a weekly reminder of my eternalness in God. I was able to view my today and the problems it held from an eternal perspective."

Mimi made a secret choice to move from knowledge (the room of understanding) to action (the room of decision), and she is so grateful for her secret choices to pursue godliness, wisdom, and contentment. She said, "You can mimic goodness but godliness cannot be imitated."

Mimi has moved steadily toward her goal, and her choice has made a significant difference. Twenty years have passed since she began her search for a fixed focus. She has moved along her "eternity line."

Mimi

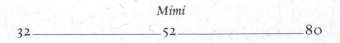

32 ——————————— 52 ——————————— 80

As Mimi's friend, I can say that today she is a woman of contentment, wisdom, and godliness. How exciting to envision the woman she will become as she progresses along toward eternity![11]

WHICH ROOM ARE YOU IN?

Now that we've looked at several women who intentionally asked God to show them what their life purpose was, I hope you're encouraged to do the same. My prayer is that you will be motivated to move from the room of understanding to the room of decision.

Each of my friends chose a God-focused purpose statement. Phyllis chose to live her life purposely, faithfully, creatively, and paradoxically. Jean visualized her life as a tree that she asked God to continually prune. Ney chose two verses and a prayer that stated her life purpose. Mimi identified who she wanted to be when she was an eighty-year-old woman, and then she identified specific steps to reach her goal.

All the women had different ways of stating their goals. Phyllis wrote out her purposes in a notebook. Ney wrote hers on her heart. Mimi's statement came after she studied some godly women. Jean's came through studying God's Word. Each woman's life goal was a process, shaped and refined over time. At some point, each made a choice to move forward with clarity and a fixed focus. In essence, each woman made the secret choice to identify, with God's help, her life purpose.

My friend, will you pray, then take pen and paper and ask God to show you your life purpose statement? Ask yourself: *Where do I want to be ten years from today?* Start with one statement or a Bible verse that describes what you believe about God and His plan for you. For example, "My life purpose is to glorify God in all I say and do." If you can't think of a verse or sentence, borrow an idea from one of my four friends (they've all given their permission). Remember, whatever you write will be a *beginning*.

Discovering their life purpose was a process for Phyllis, Jean, Ney, and Mimi; and it will be a process for you, too. But a process must have a beginning.

The following story has deeply affected my desire to live with a fixed focus. I will call this woman Mattie. Throughout her life, Mattie cherished and depended on the Word of God, committing to memory many verses from her worn King James Bible. Her life verse was 2 Timothy 1:12: "For I know whom I have believed and am persuaded that he is able to keep that which I have committed unto him against that day."

As Mattie grew older, her memory faded and details eluded her. Even the beloved faces of her family slipped from recognition. Finally, she was confined to bed in a nursing home. When her family and friends would visit Mattie, they would find her still quoting verses of Scripture, especially her well-loved life verse. But with the passing of time, even parts of this most special verse began to slip away. "I know whom I have believed," she would say. "He is able to keep . . . what I have committed . . . to Him." As Mattie grew weaker, the verse grew even shorter: "What I have committed . . . to Him."

As Mattie lay dying, her voice became so weak that her family had to strain to hear the whispered words. There was only one word left of her life verse: "Him." Mattie whispered it again and again as she neared the gates of heaven. "Him . . . Him . . . Him." He was all that was left. He was all that was needed. Her life focus was Him.[12]

VICTORIA

One more dunk of my head and I'd be finished washing my hair. Oh, the water was cold! The temperature outside had dipped to minus 5 degrees.

I was feeling sorry for myself when Victoria with the sweet smile walked through the room in her home where I was staying. I immediately felt chastened, not because of anything she said but because of who she was. I'm sure she never even noticed how icy cold the water was as she had far more difficult things to deal with than a numb scalp. What were daily inconveniences when your child was suffering? A mother's heart sees only her daughter's anguish, and little Adeana's life was one huge pain — Adeana, who wanted to follow Christ like her father and mother.

Romania in 1980 was like a prison, and Adeana, one of its young prisoners. Because her father was a pastor, Adeana was ridiculed by the teachers, made to stand before the class to be criticized and laughed at for believing in foolish myths. An aggressive child might have fought back, but Adeana's sensitive thirteen-year-old nature crumbled. Doctors prescribed heavy doses of antidepressants to treat her emotional trauma. Victoria had to watch as her most prized treasure, her daughter, became someone other than sensitive Adeana.

Is there any pain like that of a parent forced to watch a child suffer, especially when it seems like God could have intervened? I would have been full of anxiety. Victoria had learned to cast her anxieties on the One who loved Adeana even more than she did.

I wrapped a towel around my cold head and went to sit at Victoria's feet. She walked where I longed to walk — in the presence of the Sovereign King.

Worry Is Like a Rocking Chair

Worry Is Like a Rocking Chair

I collect quotes about worry. Can you identify with these?

> Worry is like a rocking chair; it will give you something
> to do but it won't get you anywhere.

> We have moments absolutely free from worry. These
> brief respites are called panic!

These sayings about worry make me laugh, but the following statements on worry make me think.

> George Müller said, "The beginning of anxiety is the
> end of faith. The beginning of true faith is the end of
> anxiety."

> All our fret and worry are caused by calculating without
> God.

When we worry, we're saying, "God can't." If we are walking in anxiety, we're not walking in faith. We want to be women of faith, yet often *worry* becomes our middle name. We know the agony of its clutches. We're familiar with the small trickle of fear that meanders through our minds until it cuts a channel into which all other thoughts are drained. We *must* conquer this "God can't" disease.

I've done a lot of thinking about worry because it's an area God is determined to work on in my life. And as I've surveyed women and asked them what they worry about, they answer *everything*! But the most prevalent worries they mention are listed below, with money being the most worrisome.

Money — How are we going to pay the mortgage this month? Can I afford to send my children to a good college? How can I afford another car?

Parenting — Will I be able to have a baby? Will I be a good mother? Will my kids put me through as much grief as I put my parents through?

Marriage — Will I ever find a man I want to marry? Will my marriage last; will it be vital? Will my husband remain faithful?

Health — Will I or someone I love get cancer or Alzheimer's?

Job security — Should I work or be a stay-at-home mom? If I work, will I keep the job?

Weight — Will I look as fat as I feel in my bathing suit?

Threats — Will I be raped? Will my child be sexually abused? Will my plane be bombed by some lunatic?

When I ask women why they worry, they give three reasons:

* The world is out of control.
* Families are out of control.
* My life is out of control.

I can identify with all these concerns, but as I look back on my life, my greatest anxieties have revolved around my four children.

SOBBING IN A NEW YORK AIRPORT

I picked up the ringing phone in our apartment in Hong Kong. It was my daughter, Robin. "Mom, something terrible is happening to my body. . . . We were at a wedding and one minute I was eating a french fry and the next, Miku (Robin's husband) was carrying me out. I was sobbing but I didn't know why. I was scared, as I could tell something was going on in my body over which I had no control. Mom, it was awful and it happened again, in the elevator. What is it? I'm so scared. My friend said it was a panic attack, but why would I have a panic attack?"

This conversation was followed by another a few weeks later.

"Mom, I have great news. I'm not having panic attacks but seizures. Isn't that great? It's not emotional, it's physical! I'm having an MRI and a CAT scan tomorrow. Aren't you glad, Mom?"

I wasn't exactly glad. Seizures in a young adult can mean lots of things, none of them too pleasant. I remember telling Jody, "Robin isn't having panic attacks. She's having seizures and she thinks that's good." I knew that seizures could mean a brain tumor, and dread began to fill my mind. My perspective wasn't helped by the fact that I had recently attended the funeral of a friend's son who had died of a brain tumor.

The trickle of fear that meandered through my mind became a torrential flood. It definitely cut a channel into which all my thoughts drained. I prayed and committed the situation to God but found myself dwelling on it five minutes later. "God, teach me to trust You," became my prayer.

Several days passed and we learned that Robin's tests showed she didn't have a brain tumor. We thanked God. The diagnosis was epilepsy, and she was put on medication to control the seizures.

My daughter was an ocean and a continent away in Philadelphia. Only a mother can understand how very far that is. I longed to see her — to hug her. Being a champion bargain hunter, I found a courier flight from Hong Kong to New York for $500 round trip and spent a week with Robin in Philadelphia. It was difficult to see the effects of the medication on her, but it seemed to be controlling the seizures. When I left on the train to catch my return flight to Hong Kong, I was grateful.

Before I boarded my plane, I called Robin because I wanted to hear her voice one last time. The voice that answered the phone was weak, barely discernible. When I said, "Honey, what's wrong?" she burst into tears. "Mom, I've had a horrible reaction to the medication. I am so sick. I've never been this sick in my life. I have a high fever, a rash all over my body, and my lymph glands are huge. The doctor says I have to go abruptly off the medication and it means the seizures will return."

As I imagined my precious daughter alone (they couldn't locate her husband at the university) and sick, I did what any self-respecting mother would do: I stood in a corner of the New York airport alone and cried my eyes out. My heart was filled with feelings of helplessness. My daughter needed me and I wasn't there.

I remembered a quote I had memorized: "Quiet tension is not trust. It is simply compressed anxiety."[1] My insides definitely felt squashed together with anxiety!

ANXIETY DEFINED

Every woman I know has, at one point or another, struggled with anxiety. I have friends who have experienced anxiety attacks due to a chemical imbalance in their brains and must be on medication to control their anxiety. This is a physical problem over which they have little control. This is not the kind of anxiety to which I am referring. I'm talking about the everyday worry we allow to control our lives.

According to Dr. Frank Minirth and Dr. Paul Meier, in their book *Worry-Free Living*, anxiety is currently the number-one mental health disorder in America.[2] Yet if you asked ten women to describe anxiety, you would get ten different answers. Here are answers from some of the women I asked to define anxiety.

- It's when I pace the floor half the night because I can't sleep.
- It's a horrible restlessness when I can't sit still, and I can't concentrate long enough to get anything done.
- It's a pain in the neck that starts in my shoulders and creeps up my neck.

These answers are all accurate, but they focus on the result of anxiety instead of defining it. So what is anxiety?

The word *worry* is derived from an old Anglo-Saxon word meaning "to strangle or choke." The stranglehold of worry keeps a woman from enjoying a life of contentment and peace.

Anxiety is that which divides and distracts the soul, that which diverts us from present duty to weary calculations of how to meet conditions that may never arrive. It's the habit of crossing bridges before we reach them.

Worry has more to do with perspective than with circumstances. In similar situations, one woman can be anxious and another peaceful. A woman worries when she perceives a threat or a danger. I use the word *perceive* because the danger can be real or imagined. When my child is standing in the middle of the street, and a car is coming, the danger is real; thus anxiety is a good thing, a warning system that will help me save my child from harm. If I worry that my child *might* take drugs, that my daughter *might* get pregnant, that my husband *might* be unfaithful, that I *might* get breast cancer, that we *might* be unable to pay our bills next month, the danger is imagined.

The French philosopher Montaigne said, "My life has been full of terrible misfortunes, most of which never happened." When we spend precious time worrying about what *might* happen, anxiety becomes negative baggage that weighs us down, saps our energy, and leaves us ineffective.

Women sometimes confuse anxiety and depression. According to Minirth and Meier, anxiety is linked more to the future, while depression is linked to the past. Depression is the past superimposed on the present, and anxiety is the future superimposed on the present.[3] One woman said that worry is the advance interest you pay on troubles that seldom come. How true, and yet we women are chronic worriers. Christian women are among the worst. *We say with one breath that we trust God and with the next breath how worried we are!* Worry and anxiety give a small thing a big shadow, and this shadow creates problems, not just in the soul and spirit, but in the body.

WORRY IS DESTRUCTIVE

It seems unbelievable, but people can literally worry themselves to death. A thirty-two-year study reported in *Circulation* found that men who were anxious were four and a half times more likely to suffer heart attacks than their worry-free counterparts. Modern medical research has proven that worry breaks down resistance to disease. More than that, it actually diseases the nervous system, and particularly affects the digestive organs and the heart. When we add to this the toll of sleepless nights and days void of contentment, we glimpse the stranglehold worry has on the human heart. Worry doesn't empty tomorrow of its sorrow, it empties today of its strength.

We know worry is destructive, and yet we continue to be choked by anxiety over what might happen. One man, looking for a solution to worry, drew up what he called a Worry Chart, in which he kept a record of his worries. He discovered that 40 percent of them were about things that probably would never happen; 30 percent concerned past decisions that he could not now unmake; 12 percent dealt with other people's criticism of him; and 10 percent were worries about his health. He concluded that only 8 percent of his worries were really legitimate![4]

Perhaps the most striking characteristic of worry is its absolute impotence. Worry never changes a single thing except the worrier. History has no record of worry warding off disaster. No tornado has been prevented, no drought averted, no plane kept from crashing, no child kept from falling off his bike, no teenager stopped from skipping classes or trying drugs. No heart attacks have ever been avoided through worry (though a great number have been caused by it). Worry is definitely counterproductive. Like our earlier illustration of a rocking chair, it doesn't get us anywhere, but at least it gives us something to do, and women like to *do* something!

How many of our hours, our days, are spent worrying about things over which we have no control and things that will never happen? There's no disputing the fact that, nine times out of ten, worrying about a thing does more damage to our body, soul, and spirit than the actual thing itself.

Is Anxiety a Sin?

Fortunately, God's Word offers a more effective cure. We can be certain there's a cure because Jesus commanded us to avoid anxiety. This is clearly seen in the warnings in the Sermon on the Mount, particularly in Matthew 6:25-34 where Jesus says, "Stop worrying."

> "Therefore I tell you, *do not worry* about your life, what you will eat or drink; or about your body, what you will wear. Is not life more important than food, and the body more important than clothes? Look at the birds of the air; they do not sow or reap or store away in barns, and yet your heavenly Father feeds them. Are you not much more valuable than they? Who of you *by worrying* can add a single hour to his life?
>
> And *why do you worry* about clothes? See how the lilies of the field grow. They do not labor or spin. Yet I tell you that not even Solomon in all his splendor was dressed like one of these. If that is how God clothes the grass of the field, which is here today and tomorrow is thrown into the fire, will he not much more clothe you, O you of little faith? So *do not worry*, saying, 'What shall we eat?' or 'What shall we drink?' or 'What shall we wear?' For the pagans run after all these things, and your heavenly Father knows that you need them. But seek first his kingdom and his righteousness, and all these things will be given to you as well. Therefore *do not worry* about tomorrow, for tomorrow will worry about itself. Each day has enough trouble of its own." (emphasis mine)

Jesus tells us *five* times in this passage to *stop worrying*. Do you think He wants us to get the message?

In these verses, Jesus labels worry, or anxiety, a sign of a faith problem. He forbids anxiety and commands us to be women of faith (verse 30). Instead of being anxious, we are to fix our focus on God and His righteousness. Verse 34 gives a key to worry-free living. *The Living Bible* makes it crystal clear: "So don't be anxious about tomorrow. God will take care of your tomorrow too. Live one day at a time." Certainly, we are to pray, plan, and prepare for tomorrow, but we are not to worry about what *might* happen. The load of tomorrow added to that of yesterday, carried today, makes even the strongest woman stumble. We are to entrust all our tomorrows to Him and live just today. Walking with God through today's twenty-four hours is difficult enough.

In *Word Studies in the Greek New Testament*, Kenneth Wuest wrote, "God commands us to 'Stop perpetually worrying about even one thing.' We commit sin when we worry. We do not trust God when we worry. We do not receive answers to prayer when we worry, because we are not trusting."[5] Bishop Fulton J. Sheen went even further when he said, "All worry is atheism, because it is a want of trust in God."[6] When I ask women if they think anxiety is a sin, they either look shocked or they gasp in disbelief. One woman said, "Well, mothers are supposed to worry."

It's easy to deceive ourselves into thinking, *I'm just concerned*, and gloss over the ugly reality that worry is sin. Worry says, "I don't trust God, I don't believe in His ability to handle my child, my marriage, my health, my job, or my loneliness." Oswald Chambers called worry infidelity: "It is not only wrong to worry, it is infidelity, because worrying means that we do not think that God can look after the details of our lives, and it is never anything else that worries us."[7]

CAST YOUR ANXIETY ON JESUS

Both Jesus and Paul commanded us to "not be anxious," but if so many people worry, and it seems so natural, how can we obey this command? The apostle Peter showed us how this is possible, and in 1 Peter 5:6-7 gave us an alternative to carrying the anxiety ourselves.

> Humble yourselves, therefore, under God's mighty
> hand, that he may lift you up in due time. Cast all
> your anxiety on him because he cares for you.

The French version says literally, "Unload on Him all your cares." The Greek word for *cast* means "to hurl." The Phillips translation of verse 7 is my personal favorite: "You can throw the whole weight of your anxieties upon him, for you are his personal concern." It is a glorious truth!

Many of us have memorized 1 Peter 5:7 and tucked it away to be pulled out whenever we have a problem. Too often, though, in applying the wonderful part about "casting all your cares," we forget the first part about "humbling ourselves under the sovereign, mighty hand of God." Not only are the two verses one thought, they are one sentence! They must be read together and applied together.

What does it mean to humble ourselves before the mighty hand of God? Humility means to have total trust in God alone. It is the surrender of our total being — intellect, emotion, will, plans, and judgments. It is relinquishing everything. For me, humbling myself involves yielding to God as the Blessed Controller of whatever situation or person is causing me anxiety.

Let's go back to the corner of the New York airport and to my moment of deep distress. No words can adequately express what I felt. I wanted to throw my plane ticket away and get back on the train and return to my daughter. I felt sick to my stomach, anxious in my spirit. I stood there distraught and sobbing. As I prayed, God brought this beautiful passage from 1 Peter 5:6-7 to mind. I had been teaching the book of 1 Peter and these verses were fresh in my heart. I prayed through them and yielded my precious daughter to Him.

Oh God, you see me here. You know my deep
pain. No words can express what I feel, but You
know. I don't understand why Robin was fine all
week and as soon as I left she became very ill, but
God, I know You are the Blessed Controller of all
things. You care personally and lovingly for my
daughter. You are intimately acquainted with all
her ways, with her brain waves, her reaction to the
medication. Father, she belongs to You. Her times
are in Your Mighty Hands. I humbly entrust her,
my precious treasure, to You, and I hurl all my
anxiety on You because You personally care for
me, just as You care for Robin.

As I prayed, a picture formed in my mind.

God, You know I am afraid of heights, but right
now I'm visualizing myself on the tallest high-rise
in Hong Kong. I am walking to the edge of the
building and I have my Robin in my arms. Holy
Father, as I look over the edge, I see You standing
below with Your arms outstretched, waiting for
me to jump, to cast all my anxiety on You. God,
I'm just one big anxiety, but I'm jumping now
into Your arms.

Twenty minutes after jumping into God's arms and unload-
ing all my cares on Him, I boarded the plane. I was at peace. I
am not by nature a peaceful person, yet I was at peace. This was a
miracle!

The episode in the New York airport was only the beginning
of trusting my daughter to the Lord. Robin and I still lived half a
world apart. During the next two years she experienced numerous
medical problems: two cancer scares, one biopsy, more medication

reactions, and uncontrolled seizures. Because of the medication, she became depressed and felt "zombie-like." She and her husband had continual financial stress and then a serious automobile accident. More stress.

What did I experience? I continually (that means over and over) had to release my daughter to God. Every time the phone rang I had to mentally fall to my knees and again release her to the Blessed Controller who loves her. Instead of worrying about her and letting my mind race with fears about what might happen, I chose to pray and ask God to watch over her. This was not easy; it was a choice I made daily, sometimes moment by moment. There was one visual aid that helped me.

MY ANXIETY BOX

Heart-shaped and tied with a ribbon, my Anxiety Box sits on the bookcase above my desk. If I shake it, I can hear the pieces of paper rustling inside. When anxiety takes over my mind, I take a small piece of paper and write out what is causing my anxiety. I date the paper and put it in my Anxiety Box. As I untie the ribbon and open the lid, I pray: "God, I am giving You this worry that's tearing me apart. As I place it in the box, I'm saying to You that it's Yours. I give it to You. You can deal with it much better than I can." I close the box, retie the ribbon, and thank God that the worry is now His.

Every time I see the box, stuffed with my worries, I'm reminded that God is carrying them, not me. Once or twice a year I open my box and read through the worries. I thank God for the ones He has taken care of. The others I put back in the heart-shaped box and entrust them to His timing.

Judy used a different kind of box to encourage her to yield her teenager to God. This huge box was beautifully and lovingly wrapped and tied with a velvet ribbon. Standing at the foot of her staircase with the box in her arms, Judy slowly walked up the stairs, saying, "God, this box represents my child — the child who has torn my heart apart. I've tried to surrender him to You, but I keep taking him back. I'm walking up these stairs and I'm leaving the box at the top. He is Yours, a gift You entrusted to me when he was born. I now, once and for all, give him back to You. Every time I walk up these stairs I will remember and thank You that he is in Your hands."

Perhaps the idea of an Anxiety Box or walking up a staircase with a huge box in your arms doesn't appeal to you. However, I challenge you to *do* something visible that encourages you to trust God.

Life is full of potential problems and pain. But we have a choice. We can worry or we can trust the Trustworthy One. We can't do both. When I feel anxious and worried about my daughter — or anything else in my life   I ask myself, "What am I trying to control instead of trusting God?"

We can benefit from those who have struggled with anxiety before us and learned the wonderful truth that God is in all our tomorrows. Listen to the words of George MacDonald.

> It has been well said that no man ever sank under the burden of the day. It's when tomorrow's burden is added to the burden of today that the weight is more than a man can bear. Never load yourselves so, my friends. If you find yourselves so loaded, at least remember this: it is your own doing, not God's. He begs you to leave the future to Him and to mind the present.[8]

F. B. Meyer made this truth plain when he said, "This is the blessed life — not anxious to see far in front, nor eager to choose the path, but quietly following behind the Shepherd, one step at a time. The Shepherd was always out in front of the sheep. He was down in front. Any attack upon them had to take him into account. Now God is down in front. He is in the tomorrows. It is tomorrow that fills men with dread, God is there already. All the tomorrows of our life have to pass Him before they can get to us."[9]

Did you catch what Meyer said? *God is already in my tomorrows, in Robin's tomorrows, in your tomorrows.* That's why we can trust them to Him and give Him the heavy load of all that *might* happen. We can leave the burden on His strong shoulders. He is much more able to carry it than we are. If we aren't worried about tomorrow, we can concentrate on trusting God for today.

FREEDOM FROM WORRY IS A PROCESS

The apostle Peter, formerly the fisherman Peter, encourages me in my journey to contentment. He is the man who instructed us to humble ourselves and trust everything to our Mighty Lord, to cast all worries into His strong arms. Yet this same Peter had been a worrier.

I think of Peter in his earlier years as "impulsive Peter, worried Peter." Walking upon the water toward Jesus, Peter became so worried that he began to sink (Matthew 14:30). He worried about who would betray Jesus; he even rebuked Jesus because he was worried that Jesus might have to suffer. Yet in his first epistle, Peter, the great worrier, tells others to hurl their anxieties on the Lord Jesus. If Peter can increase in trust and decrease in anxiety, so can you and I! It was a process for Peter; it is a process for us.

The process begins when you:

1. Acknowledge that anxiety is sin and confess it as such to God.
2. Yield to God's sovereignty. Thank Him that He is the Blessed Controller of your problems.

3. Choose to cast your anxiety on God.
4. Choose to trust God with your tomorrows and live for today.

Change My Name to "Worry-Free"

You've probably never heard of Titedios Amerimnos, but he is a man I want to emulate. We read of him in an early Greek manuscript of the Christian era. *Titedios* is his proper given name, but the second part, *Amerímnos*, is made up of the Greek word for "worry" plus the prefix meaning "not" or "never." In other words, his second name is a descriptive epithet like the second part of "Alexander the Great" or "James the Just." It is assumed that Titedios was an anxious man who became a trusting man when he met Christ and stopped worrying. So he was named "Titedios, the man who never worries."[10]

I long to have my name become "Linda, the woman who never worries." It's not as important what a woman is as what she's *becoming*, for we shall be what we are now *becoming*! If God can take a woman like me, who likes control and becomes easily anxious, and begin to transform her into a woman who is trusting God and choosing not to be anxious, He can do the same with you. Let's pray that God will change our names!

DAHLIA

Paul was definitely a catch. With good looks, brains, and brawn, he could have had his pick of young ladies, and he chose Dahlia to be his bride. Their hope was a life of service together for Christ. Never could Dahlia have imagined what lay ahead.

Paul, even in his youth, was a dynamic speaker and revered Christian leader. The problem was that Paul and Dahlia were Romanians living under a Communist regime. While the Christians respected Paul, the Securitate (secret police) plotted to destroy him.

Time after time, Paul was summoned to the police station and interrogated. House searches and constant harassment left the young family exhausted. Dahlia feared for Paul, for her children, for herself. And her fears were one day realized.

During a rainstorm, Paul looked up as he walked the narrow path around the corner of his house. Shock! Disbelief! And trembling fear. Electrical lines had been wired to the drain trough of his home — electrocution was just a few seconds and a few inches away. Only God's grace saved him from certain death. When Dahlia learned of it she cried to God, "They will stop at nothing! Must we daily live in fear of what the Securitate will do next?"

I remember a special evening with Dahlia and Paul. Before we had finished eating dinner, a man rushed in and said, "The secret police are at the hotel looking for Jody Dillow! Jody, you and Linda can't go back there. Give us your hotel key, we'll get your belongings and meet you, then you must drive for the border — fast!"

As Jody and I rushed out the door, Dahlia put her hand on my arm and smiled a smile of peace that said, "Linda, I understand. Harassment, fear, and interrogation are part of our life. Trust our Great God! He is trustworthy."

Chapter 9

Faith:
The Foundation

Faith: The Foundation

Before we go any further, it might be helpful to pause and consider the road we've traveled thus far. We began our journey in chapter one by saying that contentment is a soul sufficiency available to each of us, a peace separate from our circumstances. In chapters two through five, we looked at the areas of life where God longs for us to be content: our circumstances, ourselves, our roles, and our relationships. In chapters six through eight, we examined three barriers that keep us from being content: greed, a faulty focus, and anxiety. Now we come to a crossroads, a bridge that arches above the tumultuous waters of discontent and takes us into a new land where contentment flourishes. This bridge is called faith.

Faith raises us above our circumstances. Faith enables us to be content even when life doesn't make sense. Faith is the bulwark that keeps us strong even when we're assailed by agonizing thoughts about what might happen or by what has happened.

Faith is a vital component in our relationship with God and in our ability to be content. But what is faith, really? I asked several women in my Bible study. Here is how they defined faith:

- Faith is believing God is true to His Word when my feelings are screaming out something different.
- Faith is certain belief in what I know to be true but cannot, at that moment, feel or touch.
- Faith is completing my small part of the picture/ puzzle without being able to see the finished product.

How would you define faith? I encourage you to stop right now and write down your own definition. Not an easy task, is it? Faith is a grand concept that defies the confines of words. Still, the author of Hebrews offers a splendid definition: "Now faith is the assurance of things hoped for, the conviction of things not seen" (11:1, NASB).

These are lofty, noble-sounding words, but what are they really saying? What does it mean to be sure of what we hope for? Is there something special we're to hope for, or can we hope for anything we want? How can we be convinced about things we cannot see? And what is it that we can't see that we're supposed to be certain of?

To begin answering these questions, we must first understand the meaning of the word *assurance* as it relates to faith. In the early 1900s, scholars uncovered thousands of letters, receipts, and other documents from a two-thousand-year-old Greek colony. This word *assurance* appeared many times. Literally translated it means "title deed." A title deed is something we own. Jody and I possess a title deed to our new home. The deed says we own it; it is ours (as long as we make our monthly payments!). Likewise, faith is something we own; it is ours. But we must do more than possess faith intellectually—we must own it in our hearts. Faith is not something to be reasoned from afar, but something we throw ourselves into—heart, mind, and soul.

To better understand this, imagine yourself standing with a group of people at the top of Niagara Falls. A tightrope is stretched above the water. On the tightrope is a man with a wheelbarrow. In the wheelbarrow is a two-hundred-pound Saint Bernard dog. You watch in amazement as the man pushes the dog and the wheelbarrow safely back and forth above the falls.

After his fifth successful trip, the man turns to the crowd and says, "I can easily take a man or woman across the falls in this wheelbarrow. Do you believe this?" You think, *No problem! After all, most people would weigh less than the huge dog and wouldn't squirm so much.*

As you vigorously nod your head, agreeing that the man could do such a thing, he turns, points to you, and says, "Get in."

It's one thing to believe God can do something. It's quite another to put yourself in a position of reliant trust. This is the distinction between intellectual belief and wholehearted faith.

What would it take for you to crawl into that wheelbarrow? It would help if you were certain the wheelbarrow would hold you and the tightrope was secure. And you'd be more likely to get in if you were confident that the man pushing you was trustworthy, that he had the skill to get you across and the desire to keep you from harm. Even so, getting in the wheelbarrow would require faith.

God does not demand that you and I have *blind* faith, but *abandoned* faith, a faith that trusts Him fully. Through His Word, God willingly reveals much about who He is, what His plans are, and what He requires of us. As we come to see Him and know Him, He urges, "Trust Me." Hundreds of times in the Bible God implores us to trust Him. We tend to make trust a gray area, but with God the issue is often black and white. We either trust Him or we don't. We're for Him or we're against Him. We're in the wheelbarrow or we're on the sidelines.

As I think about true faith, heartfelt throw-yourself-in-with-complete-abandon faith, two things come to mind:

 ❧ Faith is rooted in God's character.
 ❧ Faith is based on God's Word, not on our feelings.

Let's take a closer look at each of these thoughts.

FAITH IS ROOTED IN GOD'S CHARACTER

Some people believe it doesn't matter what you have faith in, only that you believe. Thirty years ago I had a bizarre conversation with a young college student that went like this:

"It doesn't matter what I believe in," said Jenny. "It's the believing that helps me."

"Explain to me just what you mean," I replied. "What do you believe in?"

"Oh, anything. Right now I have faith in a big rock in my back yard."

"Excuse me, a big rock helps you?"

"Oh yes, if I just believe strongly enough, if I have enough faith that the rock will help me, it will. I stand in front of the big rock, close my eyes, and just believe that it will give me strength."

I explained to Jenny that the key to faith is the object of it. Christ is the trustworthy object of faith, but Jenny wanted to believe in her rock. Rocks are convenient to believe in. They expect nothing, they command nothing. No obedience is required of the "believer" in big rocks. I walked away from my conversation with Jenny knowing that she was deluded, that her "Big Rock" could not forgive her of her sin, grant her eternal life, or calm her anxious heart. Only Jesus could do that. Scripture tells us:

> The LORD is my rock, my fortress and my deliverer;
> my God is my rock, in whom I take refuge. He is my
> shield and the horn of my salvation, my strong-
> hold. (Psalm 18:2, emphasis mine)

God is worthy to be the object of our faith because of His marvelous character. Amy Carmichael, missionary to India's children, said her ability to trust God began with her confidence in God's character. Here is what she believed:

- God is, first and always, a loving Father.
- God is in control, and everything He allowed into her life was ultimately for her good.
- Like a little child, she "tucked" herself into God by

trusting Him — and He was able to carry her through all things.[1]

Confidence in God's character enabled Amy to nestle into His arms and trust Him wholly. Confidence in God's character enables us to throw ourselves with complete abandon into His care. How can we climb into the wheelbarrow if we know nothing of the One behind us?

How much easier to get in when we're confident that the One we entrust ourselves to is in control, is wise, and cares deeply for us.

GOD IS SOVEREIGN

Remember, God is the Blessed Controller of all things (1 Timothy 6:15). He has assigned us our portion and our cup (Psalm 16:5). God is in control of all the uncontrollables in our lives: What we can't see, what doesn't make sense to us, and what we don't understand. God says that He sees every tiny sparrow and counts each hair on our heads: "Are not two sparrows sold for a penny? Yet not one of them will fall to the ground apart from the will of your Father. And even the very hairs of your head are all numbered" (Matthew 10:29-30). If God has meticulously numbered each strand of our hair, He surely knows all the problems in our lives.

What God decrees for us is for our good (Ephesians 1:11; Romans 8:28). In the midst of great trouble and doubt, Job emphatically asserted, "I know that you can do all things; no plan of yours can be thwarted" (Job 42:2).

If these verses are true (and they are!) then no difficulty, pain, or trial happens to us by chance. There are no accidents, no mistakes, no miscalculations. All is under His sovereign control, and nothing is permitted but what He has decreed. And what He has

decreed is intended for our good and for His glory. His absolute
sovereignty means that I can trust Him with my tiniest doubt or
with my most heart-wrenching fear.

Knowing that God is in control makes trusting Him easier. It
also helps to know that He is wise.

GOD IS WISE

The word *wisdom* in the Bible is the translation of a Hebrew word
that means "skill." Applied to God it means that He has the skill
necessary to direct us in any and every situation. If you were sick,
who would you call, a doctor or an auto mechanic? Of course you'd
call a doctor because he would have the skill to help. He would
have the tools, the medicine, the equipment needed to make you
better. God is the Great Physician. He is Jehovah Rapha, the
Healer. He is the skillful Creator who knit you together in your
mother's womb, who formed your inward parts (Psalm 139:13). He
knows everything about you and has the skill necessary to concep-
tualize the best possible plan not only for the entire world but also
for *your* life.

Solomon tells us, "By wisdom the LORD laid the earth's foun-
dations, by understanding he set the heavens in place" (Proverbs
3:19). This being so, we can trust God, knowing that everything
that happens to us was thought out by an infinitely wise Person,
and all that happens will ultimately be for our good and His glory.

GOD IS LOVE

We affirm that God is love, but that love isn't true for us until
we personalize it in our walk with Him. God gave His life for us
as proof of His love for us. You are His child. He would do any-

thing for you. Faith in Him is so much easier when you have the confident assurance that He loves you!

> I pray that you, being rooted and established in love, may have power . . . to grasp how wide and long and high and deep is the love of Christ, and to know this love that surpasses knowledge — that you may be filled to the measure of all the fullness of God. (Ephesians 3:17-19)

Jeremiah 31:3 says that God loves you with an everlasting love. He promises that He will go before you, that He will always be with you, that He will never, never, never leave you nor forsake you (Hebrews 13:5). He says in Romans 8:38-39 that nothing, not death nor life, angels nor demons, the present nor the future — *nothing* in all of creation is able to separate you from the love of God that is in Christ Jesus.

Do you believe God loves you? You say, "I want to believe, but I can't see God. How do I know His love for me is real?" This is where faith comes in. Trust in His character. Get into the wheelbarrow, assured of what you hope for and convinced of what you do not see. Then let Him guide you along by placing your faith in the fact of His Word and in His promises, not your feelings.

FAITH IN GOD'S WORD

For the time being, let's switch our mode of transportation from a wheelbarrow to a train. Picture a bridge over Niagara Falls; that bridge is still faith. On the bridge is a train with an engine, a coal car, and a caboose. The engine represents the *fact* of God's Word, the coal car our *faith*, and the caboose our *feelings*.

It would be futile to attempt to pull the train by the caboose. In the same way, we do not depend on feelings; we place our faith in the trustworthiness of God's character and the promises of His Word.

When I read, "Heaven and earth will pass away, but my words will never pass away" (Matthew 24:35) and "The word of the Lord stands forever" (1 Peter 1:25), I realize that everything in life may change, but God's Word remains constant. I can live my life by faith, by taking God at His Word. My feelings are strong, *but*:

- God's Word is truer than anything I feel.
- God's Word is truer than anything I experience.
- God's Word is truer than any circumstance I will ever face.[2]

So how do I place my faith in the fact of God's Word and walk by faith? God's Word says, "In all things God works for the good of those who love him, who have been called according to his purpose . . . to be conformed to the likeness of his Son" (Romans 8:28-29). God declares this, but maybe my "all things" don't look so good — they definitely don't *feel* good. Regardless of what I can see or how I feel, *by faith* I choose to put the coal into the engine and not the caboose.

> God, you know my feelings are going haywire; they scream and shout that this situation is terrible and that there is no hope. God, I hope in You. I can't see what You are doing, but I trust that You're working this situation together for good. Thank You that You have promised to use it to make me more like Christ. This is what I want — it just doesn't feel good today. Give me the strength to focus my eyes on You and not on what I can see.

All of the heroes in Hebrews' faith hall of fame took God at His Word and stepped out "by faith." Let's look at one. Noah really wasn't so different from you and me. I think there must have been many days when he, too, wanted to run his train backward!

> By faith Noah, when warned about things not yet
> seen, in holy fear built an ark to save his family.
> By his faith he condemned the world and became
> heir of the righteousness that comes by faith.
> (Hebrews 11:7)

Many scholars believe that before the Flood it had never before rained on the earth. Noah lived in the middle of a desert and yet he decided to take 110 years to build a big boat because God told him there was going to be a flood. Talk about trusting God for what you can't see! What did living by faith entail for Noah?

- Working and sweating for over one hundred years without seeing any evidence of a flood.
- Hearing ridicule from the townspeople: "Hey, crazy Noah, still working on your boat?"
- Suffering the loneliness of being the only righteous man in town for over a century.

All this time Noah could not see the outcome.
I'm sure his feelings gave him problems just as ours do. Many of us have trained ourselves to live by our feelings, to give in to every impulse and emotion. As Christians we reject the "if it feels good, do it" philosophy of our society, but some of it has slowly seeped into our souls. Our pragmatic society has trained us to believe only what we can see.

The Problem: Living by Feelings
We live by our feelings and what we can see.

The Result of living by feelings? An anxious heart.

The Solution: Living by Faith
We must live by trusting God for what we can't see.
The Result of living by faith? A calm heart.

Are my eyes on Jesus or on my problem? Are my thoughts centered on the fact of God's Word or on my circumstances? These are the questions we must ask ourselves if we want to become women of contentment.

Faith looks to God, but feelings look to what is going on around us. Faith hopes in *who God is* and in *what He has promised*.

This is how Noah lived. He took God at His Word, even though building an ark in the desert made no sense, even though a century passed before he could see the reality of his faith. God commended Noah's faith and called him "an heir of righteousness." God chose him from among all the heroes of the Bible to be an example of a man who obeyed God and lived by *faith*.

Noah didn't just accept the fact of God's Word intellectually. He put "feet to his faith" and began pounding nails. With each nail he was affirming, "I believe You, God." True faith is always active. Oswald Chambers described faith as "abandoned confidence in Him."[3] It definitely took this for Noah to continue pounding nails for one hundred years.

Walking by faith is difficult because we're asked to believe what we can't see. This means we often have to walk on a dark path.

THE FAITH WALK

I asked our houseguests how they would define faith. "One step at a time on a dark path," was the answer. *How true*, I thought, *but how difficult to walk in darkness!*

Who walks in darkness and has no light? Let him
trust in the name of the LORD and rely upon his
God. (Isaiah 50:10, NKJV)

My problem is that I like light better than darkness. But if
I can see what God is doing — how He is working everything
together for good — then I don't need faith. But still I want to
see. I think we all have this problem. We say we want more
faith, but really what we want is sight. Sight says, "I see that
it's good for me, so God must have sent it," but faith says, "God
sent it, so it must be good for me." God asks us to walk by faith,
not by sight. Faith is walking in the dark with God, holding
His hand.

God doesn't keep us immune from trouble. He says, "I will
be with you in trouble." In the book of Exodus, we find the
children of Israel camped by the edge of the Red Sea. It was
night, pitch black except for the pillar of fire God had placed
between His people and the Egyptians. Can you imagine their
fear? The screaming threats of the enemy filtered through the
darkness. What would they do when dawn broke? Each mother
hugged her child to her breast in fear that this would be their
last night.

Who could have imagined the miracle that awaited them?
Hidden in the text is the tiny phrase, "All that night the LORD
drove the sea back" (Exodus 14:21). While the Israelites were
quaking in their boots, the miracle occurred "all that night."
Because it was night, they couldn't see what the "wind of God"
was accomplishing on their behalf. God parted the Red Sea,
and they walked on dry ground to freedom.

Perhaps your life is filled with darkness and you can't see.
Still, God is working, just as He worked "all that night" for the
Israelites. The next day simply manifested what God had done
during the night.[4] Do not forget, my friend, that God works in
the night of your life, too.

The city of Brussels is known for its exquisite lace. In the famous lace shops, there are certain rooms devoted to the spinning of the finest and most delicate patterns. These rooms are altogether dark, except for a light from one tiny window that falls directly upon the pattern. Only one spinner sits in the darkened room in the very place where the narrow stream of light falls upon the threads of his weaving. Lace is always more delicately and beautifully woven when the worker himself is in the dark and only his pattern is in the light.[5]

As God weaves His pattern into the fabric of our lives, sometimes we sit in a "darkened room." The darkness seems suffocating. We can't understand what He's doing and can't discover any possible good in the darkness. Yet, if we fix our focus on our faithful Weaver, we will someday know that the most exquisite work of all our life was done in those days of darkness. As I look back over my life, my deepest intimacy with Him has come from the dark times. The lessons He has burned into my heart when the black clouds hovered are the ones that have calmed my anxious heart.

Yes, faith is difficult, but our faith pleases our Holy God (Hebrews 11:6), and we do not walk the path alone. Our wise, sovereign, loving Lord walks with us. Where has God asked you to walk "by faith"? Has God asked you to trust Him with an illness, a child, a financial crisis, a husband, or lack of a husband? Do you trust in the fact of God's Word or only in what you can see? Where are your eyes? Your answers to these questions will determine whether you have an anxious heart or a heart of peace.

> *Holy Father, I am so weak. I want to trust You, but it is so hard to walk "by faith" when I can't see what You are doing. You are my Steadfast Rock. I desire to look only to You. I want to believe You for what I don't understand, what I can't see, and what doesn't make sense to me. Give me the power through Your Holy Spirit to begin pounding the nails into "my ark." May I become one who pleases You because I walk by faith.*

ILDIKO

I was nervous as I prepared for my first trip to Eastern Europe. Would I be able to relate to the women? The minute I met my translator, Ildiko, I felt at ease. As I spoke, it became clear that women are women the world over. These dear Hungarian women laughed at the same jokes and cried over the same stories I had told my American audiences. What a joy to teach with Ildiko by my side.

Over the years, Ildiko and I became friends, and I had opportunities to observe her family. Ildiko and her husband, Geza, struggled daily with relating to a totalitarian regime that denied freedoms with one hand and scheduled lives with the other. Their Christian faith was the most important thing in their life. They lived their faith and they shared the good news of Christ with others. Even little four-year-old Julia told her friends about Jesus.

One summer on a vacation in the mountains of Matra, Julia asked an older lady, "Do you know Jesus? Are you going to heaven?" The woman gasped, "Who taught you these things?" As a professor of Marxism and Leninism at the university, she was horrified that a child would be taught "foolish myths." Fear captured Ildiko's heart when she heard about Julia's discussion. What If the professor notified the authorities?

Fear continued to fill Ildiko's mind as her husband, Geza, boldly proclaimed his faith in his office at the university. And her greatest What If occurred. Geza lost his job as an engineer and became a janitor.

Now What Ifs flooded Ildiko's heart. What If she, too, lost her job? What If there wasn't enough money for the needs of her family? She decided to remain quiet about her faith.

After a few weeks, Ildiko felt ashamed that she feared man more than God and was not trusting God for her family's financial situation. She begged the Lord to forgive her: "Dear God, please give me an opportunity to speak about You to my boss." God gave her the chance a few days later.

Even though her position was changed as a result, Ildiko rejoiced. She had trusted God and conquered her What Ifs.

Trusting God with the *What Ifs*

Trusting God with the *What Ifs*

Did you know there are spiritual diseases? Two of the deadliest are the "if" diseases, *What If* and *If Only*. These illnesses are fraternal twins, alike but not alike. Both lack the eyes of faith. *What If* looks to the future and worries about what God might allow. *If Only* looks to the past and grumbles about what God has given. The first leads to anxiety, the second to anger.

Darlene longed to have a child. After years of waiting, blond, blue-eyed Amber was born. She was the perfect baby. She slept, nursed, and smiled. She was never sick, always agreeable. Angel Baby became her nickname.

As Amber grew, Darlene noticed that she seemed oblivious to others. It was as if Angel Baby lived in her own heavenly world. Amber underwent some long and agonizing testing that revealed she was autistic. Darlene and her husband went through a grieving process of understanding, accepting, then thanking God. Then they sought programs for autistic children.

Three years after Amber's birth, a brown-eyed boy joined the family. Seth was a real charmer, but was he normal? Questions stormed through Darlene's heart. I remember the day this dear, young woman looked at me and said, "Linda, is it so wrong to want to have a normal child?"

Seth was evaluated and the therapist said, "Yes, it's very possible that Seth is not normal, but we will have to wait and see."

How can one live with this kind of uncertainty, with this kind of pain? "Oh God, *What If* Seth is not normal — can I bear it? How do I wait months, not knowing? How do I trust You in the midst of this dark tunnel?" These were the cries of Darlene's heart.

Years ago I read a book called *Journey into the Whirlwind* about a Russian woman who was imprisoned for thirteen years (six in solitary confinement) under Stalin. Her crime? She was a teacher. I was so stunned by one statement in her book that I copied it and put it in my file. She said the most difficult time in her life was *not* the horrendous suffering during years of imprisonment but the three weeks of waiting prior to her arrest. The uncertainty and anxiety she felt as she and her family waited on the "unknown" was torture. Why was this? "Perhaps because waiting for an inevitable disaster is worse than the disaster itself."[1]

Waiting for the *What Ifs* of life, for what might happen, causes the sturdiest of hearts to be anxious. How did Darlene live with her huge *What If* about her son? How do you and I live with the *What Ifs* God allows in our lives? Darlene chose to look at her situation through the eyes of faith. She also worked through a practical project to help her face her worst *What If*.

MAKE THE LORD YOUR TRUST

God was teaching Darlene new and deeper lessons about trusting Him. He was also teaching me. During my time of struggling with anxiety over Robin's illness, God burned Jeremiah 17:5-8 into my heart.

> Thus says the LORD, "Cursed is the man who trusts in mankind and makes flesh his strength, and whose heart turns away from the LORD. For he will be like a bush in the desert and will not see when prosperity comes, but will live in stony wastes in the wilderness, a land of salt without inhabitant.
>
> "Blessed is the man who trusts in the LORD

and whose trust is the LORD. For he will be like a
tree planted by the water, that extends its roots by
a stream and will not fear when the heat comes;
but its leaves will be green, and it will not be anxious in a year of drought nor cease to yield fruit."
(Jeremiah 17:5-8, NASB)

These verses present us with a contrast between a man who
trusts in himself and another who not only trusts in the Lord but
also makes the Lord his total trust.

First, let's look at the woman who makes flesh her strength.
Surely, this is not a picture of me or you! We trust God! Or do we?
When we turn to control, strategies, intelligence, and manipulation, we are trusting in ourselves. Instead of giving our anxious
hearts to God, we handle the uncertainty of the *What Ifs* of life
by employing one of the control tactics mentioned above and we
"help God out." Waiting is too hard, too painful, and God just
works *way* too slow.

What's the result? Disaster. We become like the tamarisk
bush, spiritually dwarfed and with a dull, dry, lifeless appearance.
Our hearts become a desert, and we do not enjoy the prosperity of
the heart in communion with God. Our focus is on what we can
do to get what we want rather than on how we can trust.

In contrast, let's consider the woman who makes the Lord her
trust. This woman is vibrant and rich in peace. Her eyes are so
focused on her Sovereign Lord that even in a year of continual
problems she stays green and continues to bear fruit. What a glorious picture! Green leaves throughout a year of drought? No anxiety? This is what we need!

During a three-year drought God allowed in my life, this passage in Jeremiah became my prayer.

Oh God, You know my tendency to try to control and help You out. I know that "helping You

out" is what leads to an anxious heart. Forgive me. I don't want to trust in my own strength, in my strategies. I don't want to control or manipulate. Please, God, teach me what it means to not only trust You but make You my total trust. I long to become that blessed woman whose roots are planted deep by Your river. As the heat of the trials increase, I long to trust instead of fear, to be content instead of anxious. Please keep my eyes focused on You so that my leaves will stay green and fruit will be produced in the midst of the *What Ifs*.

Did God answer the plea of my heart? Yes. Did my leaves stay green? Yes. I remember going to teach a Bible study, feeling so weak in myself that I could hardly speak, and coming home overwhelmed that God had used me. I bow before Him in awe when I remember the three years of drought. During that time my picture of God enlarged by leaps and bounds.

Our Trust Level

When *What Ifs* come into our lives, we must ask ourselves if we're going to judge God by the circumstances we don't understand or judge the circumstances in light of the character of God.

Isaiah 41:10 declares, "So do not fear, for I am with you; do not be dismayed, for I am your God. I will strengthen you and help you; I will uphold you with my righteous right hand." We can only trust God when our focus is on Him and not on our circumstances.

Psalm 141:8 encourages us to fix our eyes on our Sovereign Lord and take refuge in Him. Psalm 112:7 says, "He will have no fear of bad news; his heart is steadfast, trusting in the LORD." Only as our hearts are fixed on our Sovereign, loving Lord can we be at peace in the midst of *What Ifs*. How wonderful it is to be assured that as we choose to fix our hearts on God, He, at the same time, upholds them!

Perhaps you have read these verses or even memorized them. But let me ask you, do you really trust God? This question has two possible meanings. The first is "Can you *trust* God?" Is He dependable in times of adversity? But the second meaning is also critical: "Can *you* trust God?" Do you have such a relationship with God and such a confidence in Him that you believe He is with you in your anxiety, even though you don't see any evidence of His presence and His power?

Remember: Contentment comes from a proper relationship to God, not from a response to the circumstances. Our *What Ifs* will either drive us to God and faith or they will drive us to worry and dependence on self. God gives peace and contentment; worry gives illness and misery.

PLAYING BALL WITH GOD

I will not give something I value to someone I do not trust. Before I will give my objects of anxiety to God, I must believe that He understands my problem and will handle it. I *must* believe that He has all things under His control — that He is the Blessed Controller of all things. If all things are not under His control and there are a few loose ends, and I am one of those loose ends, then my anxiety is not helped.[2]

Can you thank God that He has everything under control, that He's orchestrating all things? Your answer determines your trust level.

Most Christians are able to initially trust God with their problems. Then the doubts begin: Does God know Seth may not be normal? Does God know my daughter is ill and living in survival mode? Does God know I might have cancer? Does God know my teenager is tempted by drugs?

We find ourselves playing catch with God: *Oh God, You might drop her, let me have her back and I'll worry about her. Surely that will help.* Our trust level must be higher if we are to learn the secret of contentment. We must give the ball to God and leave it there. No more games of catch.

Are you going to judge God by the circumstances you don't understand or judge the circumstances in the light of the character of God?

Darlene's Dilemma

Let's go back to Darlene and her myriad questions. *What If* Seth is autistic? *What If* there's something else wrong with him? *What If*... As Darlene struggled with trusting Seth to God, she made a choice. She said to me, "Linda, my purpose here on earth is to glorify God. If He knows that the best way for me to bring Him glory is to have two special-needs children, then I accept His will for me."

I walked away from my discussion with Darlene humbled by her willingness to trust her greatest *What If* to God. I thought of the quote that so aptly described her: "Neither go back in fear and misgiving to the past, nor in anxiety and forecasting to the future, but lie quiet under His hand, having no will but His."[3]

Darlene chose to trust God even when she didn't understand, when she didn't feel like it, and when she couldn't see what God was doing. Working through a practical project helped Darlene face her worst *What If*. Here's what she did: "First, I asked myself, What is my worst *What If*? The answer was that Seth also would be autistic. Then I asked myself, Can I trust God with my worst *What If*? Would God still be God, would He still be Sovereign? Would He still be Love and Goodness? I answered, yes. After facing my worst *What If*, I made a decision to cast this huge anxiety on the Lord. I knew He cared for me. Then I asked God to give me the strength to live today, just today, to leave the fears and worries of tomorrow with Him."

These steps are the same ones that liberated Willis Carrier, the brilliant engineer who launched the air-conditioning industry. When Carrier was a young man, he was given a job he felt was impossible to do. He was so distraught he couldn't sleep. "My worry wasn't getting me anywhere, so I figured out a way to handle my problem without worrying." It has three steps:

1. Ask yourself what is the worst that can possibly happen.
2. Prepare to accept it if you have to.
3. Then calmly proceed to improve on the worst.

Willis Carrier said that after discovering the worst that could happen (the company would lose money and he would be fired from his job) and reconciling himself to accepting it, an extremely important thing happened. He relaxed and felt a sense of peace that he hadn't experienced in days. From that time on, he calmly devoted his time and energy to trying to improve upon the worst *What If.*[4]

The result? He solved the problem, and instead of the company losing money, it made money!

When I read this three-step plan on how to face the worst *What If,* I thought, *This seems helpful, but is it biblical?* As I searched the Scriptures, I became convinced that many people in the Bible did just what Carrier suggested. The apostle Paul said he faced death daily. He had faced the worst his enemies could do to him and was able to say, "For to me, to live is Christ and to die is gain" (Philippians 1:21). Because of this attitude, he was free to boldly proclaim the gospel. He had faced the worst and said, "It is gain," so he preached on.

Queen Esther is an example from the Old Testament. She knew that if she went before the king with her plea to revoke his order to put all Jews to death, she might die. She said, "If I perish,

I perish" (Esther 4:16). She faced the possibility of death, gave her situation to God, and then was free to devise a plan to hopefully keep the worst from happening.

Charlotte's Worst What If

My friend Charlotte found a lump in her breast. She asked herself, "What is the worst that can possibly happen?" First she thought it would be a mastectomy. Then she thought, "No, the very worst is death." So Charlotte prepared to accept death if this was what God allowed. She had asked herself, "Can I accept the loss of a breast? Yes. Can I accept death? Can I trust God to be the blessed, loving controller of this situation? Yes."

Charlotte had the mastectomy. She knew the cancer could reappear and she knew death was always a possibility, but she was at peace. To live meant seeing her grandchildren and growing old with her beloved husband. Death meant being with Christ. Because she was at peace, she was able to do everything on her part with a calm and diligent spirit — submit to surgery, maintain a strict diet and exercise routine, and rest. Charlotte amazed me by her discipline. We would be shopping in Hong Kong, finding delectable deals, and she would look at her watch and say, "Linda, it's time for my nap. I've got to go." Every day she took a nap. She determined to do her part and leave the *What Ifs* with God.

My Silly What If

Darlene and Charlotte's *What Ifs* were serious: a second autistic child and cancer. If you're like me, you occasionally get caught up in dwelling on ridiculous *What Ifs*. I feel embarrassed telling you about my fever blister *What If*, but I have strived to be honest and vulnerable in this book so far, so here goes.

In five days I was to leave for Virginia to speak at a women's retreat. A phone call informed me that before the retreat I would be interviewed by the TV anchorwoman for a two-part series on contentment. A wonderful opportunity, but there was a problem: I had a huge fever blister sticking out of my nose. *What If* it was still there on Friday? What would it look like on TV? I shuddered to think!

Several times a day I gazed in the mirror to see the progress of my fever blister. If you've ever had a fever blister, you know it can't be hurried along. Finally, I gave myself a lecture and said, "Linda, this is ridiculous! You're spending precious time caring about how you look."

So I asked myself, *What is your worst* What If? It was that my scabby fever blister would be hanging from my nose on TV. Could I accept this if I had to? Of course. I laughed at myself and told the Lord no more "mirror time" for me.

What I've been saying about dealing in a practical way with our *What If* questions is beautifully summed up in the Serenity Prayer.

> God grant me the serenity to accept that which I cannot change, courage to change the things I can, and wisdom to know the difference, living one day at a time, enjoying one moment at a time, accepting hardship as a pathway to peace, taking, as Jesus did, this sinful world as it is, not as I would have it; trusting that You will make all things right if I surrender to Your will, so that I may be reasonably happy in this life and supremely happy with You forever in the next.[5]

What are your serious *What Ifs*? What are your silly *What Ifs*? Are you ready to stop playing ball and give them to God and leave them there?

Holy Father, I cripple myself spiritually by dwelling on the What Ifs. I confess that too often I've made control and strategies my strength. You have said that blessed are those whose strength is in You. I long to be a "blessed one" who makes You, the Lord God, my total trust.

CORNELIA

During the dark years of Communist dictatorship in Romania, we watched our friends, Talosh and Cornelia, suffer. What did their suffering entail? Talosh was persecuted for being a man of God. When he was elected to a high position in the Baptist denomination, the Communists denied his election. The brave Baptists simply elected him again.

After his reelection, much to Cornelia and Talosh's surprise, the Romanian secret police invited Talosh to a fancy luncheon for a "friendly chat." They had never heard of a meeting like this. What was the purpose?

Several days after the luncheon, Talosh became ill with a minor cough and lung congestion. But as his condition steadily deteriorated, the family became concerned. When Talosh became bedridden, they realized he was dying. His doctors had no answers, so the denomination sent an American doctor to Romania to examine Talosh. The diagnosis: a yeast infection in his lungs, planted there at the "friendly lunch" by the secret police. They had infected Talosh with a slow poison!

Cornelia's prayers pounded the gates of heaven. "If only he had refused to go to the luncheon. If only the American doctor had arrived sooner. I don't understand, God. My husband loves You — he serves You. It's so hard to watch him suffer; my eyes keep slipping from You to the circumstances. Teach me how to trust You."

God loves to answer prayers like that and, over time, Cornelia's trust in God grew strong as she depended more and more on her Creator. Thankfully, the doctor was able to provide an antidote, and Talosh gradually recovered. But his illness was just one of many persecutions he was to suffer. All who knew Cornelia during the years of heartache were amazed at the serenity reflected in her face — a serenity that came from trusting God.

Trusting God with the *If Onlys*

Trusting God with the *If Onlys*

Let me tell you an old Portuguese story.

There was an old man who lived in a tiny village. Although poor, he was envied by all for the beautiful white horse he owned. Even the king coveted his treasure. People offered fabulous prices for the steed, but the old man always refused. "This horse is not a horse to me," he would tell them. "It is a person. How could you sell a person? He is a friend, not a possession. How could you sell a friend?" The man was poor and the temptation was great, but he never sold the horse.

One morning the horse was missing from the stable. All the village came to see the old man. "You old fool," they scoffed. "We told you that someone would steal your horse. You are so poor, how could you ever hope to protect such a valuable animal? It would have been better to have sold him. You could have gotten whatever price you wanted. Now the horse is gone, and you've been cursed with misfortune."

The old man responded, "Don't speak too quickly. Say only that the horse is not in the stable. That is all we know, the rest is judgment. How can you know if I've been cursed or not? How can you judge?"

The people contested, "Don't make us out to be fools! We may not be philosophers, but great philosophy is not needed to know what's happened here. The fact that your horse is gone is a curse."

The old man spoke again, "All I know is that the stable is empty and the horse is gone. The rest I don't know. Whether it be a curse or a blessing, I can't say. All we can see is a fragment. Who can say what will come next?"

The people of the village laughed. They had always thought the man to be a fool; if he wasn't, he would have sold the horse and lived off the money. Instead, he was a poor woodcutter, living hand to mouth in the misery of poverty. Now he had proven that he was, indeed, a fool.

After fifteen days, the horse returned. He hadn't been stolen, he had run away into the forest. Not only had he returned, he had brought a dozen wild horses with him. Once again the village people gathered around the woodcutter and spoke, "Old man, you were right and we were wrong. What we thought was a curse was a blessing. Please forgive us."

The man responded, "Again, you go too far. Say only that the horse is back. State only that a dozen horses returned with him, but don't judge. How do you know if this is a blessing or not? You see only a fragment. Unless you know the whole story, how can you judge? If you read only one page, how can you judge the whole book? All you have is a fragment! Don't say that this is a blessing. No one knows. *I am content with what I know. I am not perturbed by what I don't know.*"

"Maybe the old man is right," they said. But down deep they believed he was wrong. They knew it was a blessing. Twelve wild horses had returned with one horse. With a little bit of work, the animals could be broken and trained and sold for much money.

The old man had a son, an only son. The young man began to break the wild horses. After a few days, he fell from one of the horses and broke both legs. Once again the villagers gathered around the old man and cast their judgments.

"You were right," they said. "The dozen horses were not a blessing. They were a curse. Your only son has broken his legs, and now in your old age you have no one to help you. Now you are poorer than ever."

The old man spoke again, "Don't go so far in your judgments. Say only that my son broke his legs. Who knows if it is a blessing or a curse? No one knows. We only have a fragment of the whole."

A few weeks later the country engaged in war against a neighboring country. All the young men of the village were required to join the army. Only the son of the old man was excluded because he was injured. The enemy was strong and the people feared they would never see their sons again. Once again, they gathered around the old man, crying and screaming because their sons had been taken. "You were right, old man," they wept. "God knows you were right. This proves it. Your son's accident was a blessing. His legs may be broken, but at least he is with you. Our sons are gone forever."

The old man spoke again, "Why do you always draw conclusions? No one knows. Say only this: Your sons went to war, and mine did not. No one is wise enough to know if it is a blessing or a curse. Only God knows."[1]

The old woodcutter was content with what he knew and not disturbed by what he couldn't understand. Epictetus said, "I am always content with that which happens, for I think that which God chooses is better than what I choose."

If we are to find contentment in the midst of trial and uncertainty, we must accept our situation as being purposely allowed into our lives by a personal and loving God. For most of us, this begins by refusing to contract the *If Only* disease.

Avoiding the *If Onlys*

Jim refused to contract the *If Only* disease, even though he was constantly exposed to it. Jim and his family had left everything to go to Africa as missionaries. While there, Jim contracted a virus similar to chronic fatigue syndrome. He has been sick for twelve years. For six of those years he was bedridden. He has consulted thirty-five doctors on three continents without finding a cure, and he is only able to work limited hours.

This dear family visited us last summer. While Lois and the girls toured Colorado Springs, Jim stayed in our basement and read. Occasionally he joined his family, but he could climb the stairs only once a day and had to conserve his energy. This is after *twelve* years of suffering. One might think bitterness, self-pity, impatience, and anger would characterize this man. But that's not what I saw. His physical disease didn't cause him to think, *If Only we hadn't gone to Africa.* He was at peace with what God had allowed. Lois told me that once, during his six-year stint in bed, she asked Jim, "Don't you ever feel sorry for yourself?" He responded, "Pitying oneself takes too much energy. I don't have any energy to spare."

How much time do we spend in self-pity, thinking, *If Only my situation were different?* Jim didn't allow himself the luxury of *If Onlys.* He was content with what God had allowed in his life.

Recorded in the wonderful little book *Green Leaf in Drought* is a saga of *If Onlys.* When the Communists ordered all missionaries out of China in 1947, Arthur and Wilma Matthews had just traveled to a remote part of China and were prohibited from leaving. As all their colleagues escaped, the *If Onlys* plagued their hearts and minds. "*If Only* that letter had not come, inviting us here. *If Only* Arthur had not signed that petition for world peace, which angered the authorities. *If Only . . .*"

Wilma became so distraught over their situation, so paralyzed by the *If Onlys*, that on Easter she could not sing "He Lives." She felt God had deserted them. Alone in her drab kitchen, she turned to a pamphlet by A. B. Simpson titled, "The *If* in Your Life." She read the account of Lazarus's death and how Martha had said to Jesus, "Lord, *If Only* You had been here, my brother would not have died." And Jesus could have been there; He was not far away. He knew all about it and He let Lazarus die.

Wilma realized a great truth: There's an *if* in every life — something God could have done differently *if* He had chosen to do so. He has all power, yet He often allows that *if* to be there. God wanted to meet Wilma's *if* with His *if*, just as He had for Martha. Jesus told Martha, "Did I not tell you that *if* you believed, you would see the glory of God?" (John 11:40). Martha wanted Lazarus to be delivered *from* death; Christ wanted Lazarus to be triumphant *over* death.[2]

Two years later, the Matthewses were allowed to leave China. Despite severe testing and horrible circumstances, they deliberately chose not to think about the *If Onlys* and to focus instead on God's Loving Sovereignty. As a result they had internal peace, and God was glorified.

We cripple ourselves spiritually by going over and over the *If Onlys*. We "catch" the *If Only* disease when we dwell on what we don't have instead of on what we do have. We become discontented with what God has given us. When we contract this disease, we lose perspective. Consider the Israelites.

> In the first month the whole Israelite community arrived at the Desert of Zin, and they stayed at Kadesh. There Miriam died and was buried.
>
> Now there was no water for the community, and the people gathered in opposition to Moses and Aaron. They quarreled with Moses and said, "*If Only* we had died when our brothers fell dead before the LORD! Why did you bring the LORD's community into this desert, that we and our livestock should die here? Why did you bring us up out of Egypt to this terrible place? It has no grain or figs, grapevines or pomegranates. And there is no water to drink!" (Numbers 20:1-5, emphasis mine)

The Israelites had a problem: no water. (Usually the *If Only* disease comes as a result of a real problem.) Instead of focusing on God, they focused on the problem. This led to irrational thinking. They lost all perspective and began to look back on Egypt with longing. This is unbelievable! They hated Egypt when they lived there. As slaves they had been forced to create bricks without straw and suffered many other persecutions.

When the Israelites dwelt on what they didn't have, their one problem mushroomed until they had compiled a long list of grievances. "*If Only* we were back in Egypt. *If Only* we had vines, figs, and yummy things to eat. Manna is boring." At the end of their list, they finally added the real problem, "nor is there water to drink."

I can identify with this process of multiplied gripes. My mind is expert at taking one negative and ballooning it into many until I have enough balloons to throw a pity party. That's what the Israelites were doing. Their complaints dropped like confetti.

These were the same people who had seen the ten plagues come on Pharaoh and who had witnessed the miraculous opening of the Red Sea. When they had no food, God had fed them by sending manna. Day after day, for *forty* years, Jewish housewives collected God's provision. You'd think they would have celebrated not having to shop, cook, or clean, yet here they were grumbling in unbelief over "no water." They had completely lost sight of God's faithfulness.

Certainly their need for water was a legitimate concern, but the Israelites' eyes were on the problem and not on the Problem Solver. If God could cause the water of the Red Sea to part, surely He could provide a little drinking water. But their eyes were fixed on the problem, not on the God of miracles.

Numbers 20:12 relates how God responded to the continual complaints: Moses and Aaron would not lead the people into the Promised Land. Why? "But the LORD said to Moses and Aaron, 'Because you did not trust in me enough to honor me as holy in the sight of the Israelites, you will not bring this community into the land I give them.'"

Our faith is a serious issue with God. He wants us to trust Him, no matter what our situation is, no matter what our portion. This was extremely difficult for my friend Darla.

ACCEPTING GOD'S PORTION FOR YOU

Several years ago I received the following letter from Darla.

> Ours was a storybook romance. Rob was the person God had chosen for me and I knew our marriage would last forever. We had known each other since childhood and our wonderful friendship blossomed into a special romance.
>
> Stark reality hit our "happily ever after" fourteen years later. I discovered Rob in our bed with a young friend of ours. There are no words in the English language to express the sorrow, the pain, the devastation. My life drained away as I viewed the scene in *my* bed with *my* husband and *my* friend. It appeared that my husband, who believed in Christ, also believed in adultery.
>
> When Rob asked for forgiveness, promising it would never happen again, I forgave him and believed our marriage could recover and even become stronger. I knew our young boys needed their father, and I still loved and needed Rob.
>
> The next years were a roller coaster for me. Rob's middle name is "charming." He is the all-time consummate liar, and I believed him.
>
> A year ago I again discovered he was involved with another woman and asked him to move out. Embarrassment and shame plagued me. Now everyone would know, including our sons. We had both been active in our church, taught Bible studies, and discipled people. What would people say about our Christian testimony?
>
> My human support system was stripped away, and I found myself alone with two hurt and angry

teenage boys whom I was responsible to guide into manhood. I felt so alone; I had lost control of my life. Sometimes my brain felt so numb and foggy that I was incapable of performing the sim-' plest tasks. I clung to God with all my might, all the while asking Him many questions: "*If Only* this marriage mess would disappear! How could it be Your will for us to divorce when You hate divorce? You are all powerful; why don't You change Rob?"

The end of my storybook romance is still unknown. I have no answers as to why God allowed this in my marriage, but God has taught me much. I have learned that I can only be responsible for me. I can't make my husband's choices; only he can. I am willing to accept whatever God has for me, either singleness or reconciliation.

Recently I received another letter from Darla and marveled at her continual growth. She said, "I'm trying to learn obedience and acquiescence to God's will in the tiniest details of my life. I don't want to waste any more of my life being sad and nonfunctioning because of my situation with my husband." Darla is choosing to trust God with her portion.

While I haven't walked in Darla's shoes, I have struggled to accept my portion. Part of God's portion for me right now is a weekly visit to a chiropractor and a neuromuscular massage therapist. Because we live in the country, each visit takes two to three hours. It was not my plan to be rear-ended on the freeway and to be the recipient of whiplash, but it was my portion. God allowed the accident, therefore I can choose to be content with discomfort and a revised schedule, or I can grumble and increase the tension in my body. It's a little thing. What is whiplash compared to Jim's suffering, to the death of a child, to an unfaithful husband, to the unspeakable pain experienced daily by many? Insignificant. A small thing. Nothing — yet this "nothing" has disrupted my life. Often it is the "nothings" that cause us to grumble and be discontent.

Peace comes through acceptance.

REMEMBERING THE DEEDS OF THE LORD

We survive the packages of pain God allows in our lives by remembering who God is and what He has done in the past. When *If Onlys* invade my mind, when anguish fills my heart, I return to one of my favorite psalms. It is a place where God has met me time after time. Read Psalm 77 and hear the psalmist's pain-drenched words: "My soul refused to be comforted. I remembered you, O God, and I groaned; . . . I was too troubled to speak. . . . Has his unfailing love vanished forever? Has his promise failed for all time? Has God forgotten to be merciful?" (Psalm 77:2-4,8-9).

These questions sound like my questions. But listen to how the psalmist's despair changes from pity to praise.

> I will remember the deeds of the LORD; yes, I will remember your miracles of long ago. I will meditate on all your works and consider all your mighty deeds. Your ways, O God, are holy. What god is so great as our God? You are the God who performs miracles; you display your power among the peoples. (Psalm 77:11-14)

I will remember. This is a key to trusting God. Many nights I have gotten out of bed, taken paper and pen in hand, and forced myself to remember what God has done in the past, to remember His faithfulness to me. As I list all God has done, it helps me to trust Him in the present. One dark night I wrote in my journal:

It is 1 a.m. — my body, my soul are tossing and
turning — my mind is on fire with If Onlys, What
Ifs, and Whys. I feel like I will explode. I go to the
Word and read, "Why art thou cast down, O my
soul, and why art thou disquieted in me?" I love
the old translation of this verse: "Why droopest
thou, O my soul, and frettest so upon me?" This
describes me — a droopy soul. I read, "Hope thou
in God for I shall yet praise Him for the help of
His countenance." I know I need to focus on God
and take Him at His Word — I know I shouldn't
listen to my feelings.

But my soul droops yet again — my mind fixes
again on the problem instead of on the Living
God. I feel like screaming. No matter what I fix
my mind on, it circles back to the pain. "O God,
my soul is so droopy, turn my eyes to You and
Your faithfulness."

I will remember Your work in the past, Your
faithfulness. I know the only way to remember is
to detail Your faithfulness. I'll make a list to help
me remember.

Andrew Murray made a list "to remember." His words put
dark days and nights in perspective. In 1895 he was in England
suffering from a terribly painful back, the result of an injury
incurred years before. One morning, while he was eating breakfast
in his room, his hostess told him of a woman downstairs who was
in great trouble and wanted to know if he had any advice for her.
Andrew Murray handed her a paper he had been writing on and
said, "Give her this advice I'm writing down for myself. It may be
that she'll find it helpful." This is what he wrote.

In time of trouble, say, "First, he brought me here. It is by his will I am in this strait place; in that I will rest." Next, "He will keep me here in his love, and give me grace in this trial to behave as his child." Then say, "He will make the trial a blessing, teaching me lessons he intends me to learn, and working in me the grace he means to bestow." And last, say, "In his good time he can bring me out again. How and when, he knows." Therefore, say, "I am here (1) by God's appointment, (2) in his keeping, (3) under his training, (4) for his time."[3]

Andrew Murray chose not to focus on the problem and say, "*If Only* I wasn't suffering with this pain." His focus was on God and His purposes. I memorized this quote so that whenever I'm tempted to slide down into the mire of *If Only* thinking, I'm reminded to go to the Problem Solver with my concerns. Instead of getting worried and anxious, I pray about my problem.

What are your *If Onlys*? Will you pray this prayer and yield your *If Onlys* to the One who holds your hand and all your *Ifs* in the palm of His hand?

Holy Father, forgive me for grumbling. I know I've sounded just like the Israelites. I long to dwell not on the If Onlys but on You. Make me wise like the old woodcutter — content with what I know, not perturbed by what I don't know.

MONIQUE

Monique's eyes were swollen shut. She couldn't stop sobbing. "No, God, You can't mean this! Why, God? My heart feels like it is being ripped in two. Are you truly asking me to leave my son here in China? Why, God? You gave him to me — why are You taking him back?"

Monique and Christophe had adopted a two-year-old Chinese boy and named him Jean Paul fifteen years before. He was an orphan and they were his only family. He needed them! His faith was not strong enough. What would happen to him? While her mother's heart was breaking, Monique knelt before the Lord and prayed, "Oh, God, I don't understand but I give my son to You. Be his mother, his father, his all." Because her son was Chinese, Monique had to leave Jean Paul behind in China when the family returned to France.

That happened in 1949, when the Communists forced all missionaries out of China. In 1988, Jody and I were in China and we met Jean Paul and heard his story. After his adopted parents were forced to leave, he fell in love with the Lord Jesus. He married, had children, and became a vocal advocate for the cause of Christ. Because of his faith, he was imprisoned for twenty-one years. While he was in prison, the Communists convinced his wife that he was a traitor, and she divorced him. He never saw his wife or children again.

Everyone he loved had been torn from him, yet Jean Paul chose to trust God. He became a traveling teacher, ministering to thousands in the house church movement in China. As we talked, he was hiding from the secret police.

Jean Paul could have spent all his time asking Why. Yet he glowed; there is no other word to describe his countenance.

Monique never saw her son again. She died not knowing how God had answered her prayers. Today, in heaven, I am sure she's rejoicing.

Chapter 12

———

Trusting God with the *Whys*

❧

Trusting God with the *Whys*

Frau Braun smiled as she handed me the contract — several single-spaced, typewritten pages. As I waded through the German words, I thought, *This is incredible.* We had been told when we rented the apartment that we would not have to sign a contract, that Herr and Frau Braun *liked* teenagers. Now we had uprooted our family from Vienna, moved twelve hours away to this small town in Germany, and discovered that we would have to sign a contract.

Some of the conditions were:

- If someone has a birthday and you sing "Happy Birthday," don't sing too loud or too long.
- If you use a sewing machine, turn it to the lowest noise level. (Since sewing is at the bottom of the list of things I do, I didn't even know sewing machines had noise levels.)
- Don't have company often.

The contract went on for four pages. Was this for real? Did renting an apartment entitle the owner to legislate your lifestyle?

Clearly, teenagers upset the Brauns, and they expected them to always be quiet (an impossibility for my creative, laughing, and just plain loud teens). We had come to Germany to rest. Jody and I were exhausted from eight years of travel and ministry in Eastern Europe and Russia. Our teens were excited about going to the Christian school in this small town. The Brauns' fully furnished three-bedroom apartment had seemed an answer to prayer.

The contract was the first hint that difficult times lay ahead. We had thought this year would be a carefree Sunday drive. Instead, we were beginning to feel like we were driving a vehicle with a broken steering rod — on a crooked road.

THE CROOKED AND THE STRAIGHT

I personally prefer the "straight" times! I like to be able to see how everything is fitting together. The crooked times are difficult, not just because they're crooked but because we can't see how God is working. But those are the times that require faith. Remember, God is fitting things together even when we can't see. It just doesn't feel as good or as safe. The book of Ecclesiastes encourages us to rejoice when life is easy and to trust God when it isn't.

> Consider the work of God, for who is able to straighten what He has bent? In the day of prosperity be happy, but in the day of adversity consider — God has made the one as well as the other so that man may not discover anything that will be after him. (Ecclesiastes 7:13-14, NASB)

Myrna Alexander, in her excellent Bible study *Behold Your God*, offers some insight into what this means.

> There is the crooked that God causes and the crooked that we create for ourselves and God allows. We make mistakes, blunders, messes. We can create disorder, chaos, sadness, and suffering by breaking God's instructions concerning how life is to be lived. Yet He who is in control over all things says, concerning the seemingly crooked that He has made or the crooked we have caused,

"All things work together for good to them that
love God, to them who are the called according to
His purpose."[1]

Frau Braun and her unreasonable contract presented us with a
crooked situation. After four days of praying about what I should
say (my dear husband said I should be the one to talk to her because
my German was better than his), I ventured downstairs to nego-
tiate. Frau Braun assured me that the contract was only a
formality.

I hoped we were understanding one another, and I asked her
to please let me know if we were doing anything that bothered
them.

As the weeks passed, it became obvious that Herr Braun was
a sick man, full of anger and vindictiveness. One day Frau Braun
was ill and I took dinner to her. As I was leaving, Herr Braun
stormed in yelling. No, yelling isn't a strong enough word — he was
violently screaming. I was thankful I didn't understand all he was
saying to us, but I did understand that he was angry because our
son, Niki, had left the front door open. Never had I been treated
like this. I was shaking as I walked up the stairs alone. My "spiritual" thought was that I hoped he would choke on the nice dinner
I had spent the morning cooking for them.

Bad became worse when Herr Braun pounded on our door
at 10 p.m., furious because I was taking a bath. The water running down the pipes bothered them! This time he yelled at Jody (I
stayed in the bathtub!). He screamed that we were to get out, that
the contract was broken. We were to leave as soon as possible. But
where would we go? There were few rentals in this village of five
thousand people, but we traipsed out in the snow to search.

We needed a furnished place for five. The only place available was a *Ferien Wohungen*, a vacation home. We had to pay by the
day, and the rent was almost three times what we had paid at the
Brauns'. Though it was okay to live in for a week, as a long-term

rental the apartment could be classified as a pit.

It smelled like a brewery, and when Jody hooked up a washing machine (no dryer) in the basement, we discovered why. Our new landlord (who was a dear man) made schnapps in the basement. All year I watched (and smelled) the fermentation process while I did my fifteen to twenty loads of laundry each week. I was surprised my clothes didn't stand up by themselves after being washed near the brew and then strung over the heaters to dry. Jody was continually offered schnapps (as early as 10 a.m.), and the landlord finally told him, "Herr Dillow, didn't you know the Bible says it is good to drink schnapps two times a day?" Jody and I searched the Scriptures but figured he must have been talking about a different Bible.

Friends told us, "This place looks like it belongs in a third-world country. If you pay over $350 rent a month, it's a rip-off." (It definitely was!) But we learned to live together in closeness and decided it wasn't too bad. Then one day while sitting in my kitchen I looked up, and there, growing out of a crack in my ceiling, were mushrooms! What a creative God we have. Yes, we had an "early attic" vacation home with exorbitant rent, *but* He was supplying us with free vegetables!

The positives were our wonderful friends, a very special Christian school, and a nice, schnapps-making landlord. The negative was the continued harassment from Herr Braun. Angry, derogatory letters from him frequented our mailbox, accusing us of breaking things and leaving the apartment unclean. The latter accusation especially riled me as I had spent an entire day cleaning every corner. Finally, we had to get a lawyer to settle the financial issues.

We had come to this town to rest, but it was not restful. "Why, God?" I asked.

HABAKKUK: A MAN WITH A CROOKED SITUATION

When women ask me my favorite book of the Bible and I answer, "Habakkuk," I get some strange looks. God has used the testimony of this dear man to encourage me, to exhort me, and to show me what it means to trust God with my *Why* questions. The book of Habakkuk is short — only three chapters — and is simply a record of communication between the prophet and God.

Habakkuk was different from the other Old Testament prophets who addressed either their own countrymen or a foreign people. Habakkuk talked to God alone. He was a man with a crooked situation. After the death of Josiah, the last godly king, the people worshiped false gods, and very little honor was given to Yahweh.

Moral corruption was rampant in Judah, yet God was silent. Violence and lawlessness raged; God seemed unconcerned. It appeared that God was not working. Habakkuk came before God and asked the age-old questions that tear our hearts apart: "How long, O Lord?" "*Why*, God? *Why* do You allow evil and wickedness to continue in Judah?" He prayed:

> How long, O LORD, will I call for help,
> And Thou wilt not hear?
> I cry out to Thee, "Violence!"
> Yet Thou dost not save.
> Why dost Thou make me see iniquity,
> And cause me to look on wickedness?
> Yes, destruction and violence are before me;
> Strife exists and contention arises.
> Therefore, the law is ignored
> And justice is never upheld.
> For the wicked surround the righteous;
> Therefore, justice comes out perverted.
> (Habakkuk 1:2-4, NASB)

God answers and says He will do something that Habakkuk
would not believe. Habbakuk starts to yell, "Hurrah!" but stops
dead in his tracks. What is God saying?

> "For behold, I am raising up the Chaldeans,
> That fierce and impetuous people
> Who march throughout the earth
> To seize dwelling places which are not theirs.
> They are dreaded and feared.
> Their justice and authority originate with them-
> selves." (Habakkuk 1:6-7, NASB)

Habakkuk was in shock. God's answer created an even
bigger problem. Judah deserved punishment, but *Why* would
God punish Judah by sending the Chaldeans, who were far
more wicked and ruthless than the Judeans? To Habakkuk's
mind, they would make matters worse, not better. It made no
sense. What kind of a plan was this? Any child could think up a
better one.

To understand Habakkuk's distress, let's put his situation
into a contemporary context. Many people today are concerned
about the growing violence in the United States. Every day we
read about crime, drugs, alcoholism, and the murder of babies
through abortion. Women fear going out at night, and parents
have to be cautious about who is caring for their children. Rape,
sexual abuse, and perversion have escalated to mammoth pro-
portions. Like Habakkuk, we wonder if justice is paralyzed, as
it often seems to come out perverted. Hearts ache over what is
happening, and so we gather to pray as Habakkuk prayed: "How
long, O Lord? *Why*, God, do You allow this evil wickedness to
permeate our country? Do something, God!"

Imagine our response if God answered by saying, "Look, be
astonished and wonder! I am doing something in your days you
would not believe if you were told. For behold, I am raising up

Osama bin Laden, that evil terrorist, to take over America."

We would cry out, "Excuse us, God, surely we misunderstood. You couldn't possibly mean that You are sending this incarnation of Satan to judge America. We're bad but not *that* bad."

We would be horrified at the thought. Well, that's how Habakkuk felt.

The reputation of the Chaldeans would have caused anyone major distress. We read in Habakkuk 1:6-11 that they were a fierce and impetuous people who seized what belonged to others; they were feared; their authority and justice originated with themselves. They were excellent horsemen who flew like eagles and swooped down to devour. Their whole purpose was centered in violence, and they collected captives like sand. They mocked kings, laughed at fortresses, and their strength was their god. No wonder Habakkuk didn't understand. But instead of wailing, "That's not fair!" he appealed to God's character — His holiness and purity — and asked God *Why*.

> Art Thou not from everlasting,
> O LORD, my God, my Holy One?
> We will not die. . . .
> Why art Thou silent when the wicked swallowed up
> Those more righteous than they?
> (Habakkuk 1:12-13, NASB)

After asking his questions, Habakkuk said, "I will stand on my guard post and station myself on the rampart; and I will keep watch to see what He will speak to me, and how I may reply when I am reproved" (Habakkuk 2:1). In other words, he would wait until he heard God's reply to his concerns.

Some people believe God doesn't speak to us today as He did long ago. I disagree. The truer statement is that we don't listen and wait as Habakkuk did. We don't know how long he waited, but we do know God answered him.

Then the LORD answered me and said,
"Record the vision and inscribe it on tablets,
That the one who reads it may run.
For the vision is yet for the appointed time;
It hastens toward the goal, and it will not fail.
Though it tarries, wait for it;
For it will certainly come, it will not delay.
Behold, as for the proud one,
His soul is not right within him;
But the righteous will live by his faith."
(Habakkuk 2:2-4, NASB)

God reaffirmed that what Habakkuk had heard was true — the Chaldeans were coming — *but* Habakkuk was to live by faith. This same statement is repeated three times in the New Testament: "The just shall live by faith" (Romans 1:17; Galatians 3:11; Hebrews 10:38). In other words, God didn't explain *Why*; instead He told Habakkuk to trust Him with all his *Whys*. Habakkuk was to trust God for what he didn't understand, what he couldn't see. He was to walk in the dark with God.

From a human perspective, this answer is frustrating. We want to know *Why*. Surely God should explain Himself to us. Sometimes He does, but often He does not. God is God and He doesn't need to explain Himself. If we could fully comprehend God, He wouldn't be God — He would be like us. In those instances when God doesn't tell us *Why*, we will have to wait until we're in heaven for our answers.

Habakkuk realized this. Although he didn't get the response he wanted, he affirmed that God is God, in spite of Habakkuk's human lack of comprehension. Habakkuk praised God in his spirit, yet in his body he was quaking in his boots! "I heard and my inward parts trembled, at the sound my lips quivered. Decay enters my bones, and in my place I tremble. Because I must wait quietly for the day of distress, for the people to arise who will invade us" (Habakkuk 3:16, NASB).

I love this description of this dear saint — trembling, in agony of spirit, in so much pain that he said his bones were decaying! This encourages me, as my body often rebels when I'm trying to trust in my spirit. And even though his body and soul were quaking, Habakkuk declared what I believe is the most beautiful proclamation of faith in the Bible.

> Though the fig tree should not blossom,
> And there be no fruit on the vines,
> Though the yield of the olive should fail,
> And the fields produce no food,
> Though the flock should be cut off from the fold,
> And there be no cattle in the stalls,
> Yet I will exult in the LORD,
> I will rejoice in the God of my salvation.
> The Lord GOD is my strength,
> And He has made my feet like hinds' feet,
> And makes me walk on my high places.
> (Habakkuk 3:17-19, NASB)

What an incredible statement of trust in God! Though Habakkuk be brought to utter destitution, yet he will rejoice. Though everything is taken away — including the crops and cattle that provided him with food and drink — he will trust in the Lord, his strength. His words literally mean, "I will jump for joy in the Lord. I will spin around for delight in God."[2] Joy at its best, with circumstances at their worst.

What, then, was Habakkuk's process as he moved from his sob of doubt to this song of trust?

- He told his honest doubts to God.
- He resolved to wait on God.
- He chose to trust God in the dark.

I shared with you my account of a year with a crotchety landlord. It was a difficult year, but not nearly as difficult as the pre-
ceding year that had caused us to move to Germany and put our
children in the Christian school. Habakkuk's burden was such an
"other-centered" burden — concern for his country and the spiritual well-being of his people. My burden was more personal.

MY CROOKED SITUATION

Vienna was not my choice of a good environment in which to raise
my children. When we moved there, the children were in elementary school. On one of our first trips to the grocery store, my son
Tommy pointed to a music cover displaying full frontal nudity and
said, "Mommy, *look!*" Mommy didn't want to look or have her son
look!

Prostitution is legal in Austria. I remember driving down a
main street with the children to pick up guests at the train station.
The prostitutes were standing on the street corners in outland-
ish attire (this is a kind description). As we drove, my daughter
Joy was counting the prostitutes — "nineteen, twenty, twenty-
one . . . oh, look, Mommy, she got someone." I felt sick to my stomach. Exposure to nudity and prostitution had not been in my plans
for my children. Even with these problems, I felt I was able to protect my children to some degree.

When they became teenagers, I had more difficulty protecting them. There were four teenage girls from missionary families
in the American high school. We mothers were so thankful they
could encourage each other and hold one another up. It sounded
good but wasn't to be. The pressure was too great. The legal
drinking age in Austria is fifteen; beer is served at McDonald's
along with hamburgers and fries. All the swimming pools and
beaches on the Danube River were topless, so we didn't allow
our teens to go swimming. When I wouldn't allow them to see

movies with nudity, how could I let them see nudity up close and personal?

One mother and I prayed weekly for the teenage girls, as they tried to keep their values. As we prayed we watched her daughter struggle and become bulimic under the pressure. The family returned to the States, along with several other missionary families with teens. Jody and I didn't know what to do. We couldn't accept that having teens meant you had to leave the mission field. But neither were we prepared to sacrifice our children on the altar of our ministry in Eastern Europe. During the summer, we went camping alone for a week to seek God's wisdom. "Do we leave our children in this environment? Do we return to the States? Help, God!"

After praying for a week, we still weren't sure what to do. It would have been nice if God had told us by writing on the wall of the camper, but no writing appeared, no "good feeling." I told Jody he should make the decision. I was too emotional to trust what I thought. He decided that we should trust our children to God and stay and minister in Eastern Europe. I was scared, and so was he.

An hour after we returned home, the phone rang. It was one of the mothers who had gone to the States. She was calling to tell me they were not returning to Austria. "Linda, when the elders of our church heard about the environment for our daughter in Vienna, they encouraged us not to take her back there. My husband is returning to pack up and ship everything back to the United States."

I hung up the phone and said, "Excuse me, God, we prayed and we think You want us to keep our daughter in this environment. They prayed and a whole group tells them to leave! I'm terrified. But, Lord, I will stay here and be a missionary for You. I only ask You one thing. Please protect my child."

During the next months, I watched as my child fell apart, crumbling under depression. An excellent student, she fell from an A to an F in math. Something was definitely wrong. My happy child who always smiled quit smiling. As my daughter spiraled down, so did I.

By spring I was at the lowest point in my life, physically, emotionally, and spiritually. I had trusted God with my most precious treasure and it appeared He had let me down. During this time, a businessman visiting from Texas told us, "This ministry is the most exciting I have ever observed in any country." I wanted to scream, "But at what cost!" If a plane had landed in my backyard I would have grabbed my children and flown away. I had never really doubted God. Now I was besieged with questions. I doubted God's goodness and His sovereignty. I couldn't open my Bible. It was full of promises, yet they didn't seem to apply to me, to my child.

Jody said to me one day, "Where else can we go? He has the words of eternal life." In my heart I knew he was right. I began to ask myself the question, "Am I going to judge God by circumstances I can't understand or judge the circumstances in the light of the character of God?" I opened my Bible and began to study Habakkuk: Oh, how I identified with his questions! I read and reread his story. I realized I must ask God all my questions and then station myself on the ramparts to wait for His answer.

God did not tell me Why. This side of heaven I may never know Why events happened as they did. God's answer to me was His answer to Habakkuk, "The righteous shall live by faith." I knew I had to believe, even when I couldn't see, or else it wasn't faith. I had to trust God for what I didn't understand, what didn't make sense to me. I had to walk in the dark with God, holding on to His hand.

I grabbed my Bible and went out on the balcony with a piece of paper and a pen. The apple trees were in bloom, and the aroma was overwhelmingly lovely. It was 1984, but I can remember it as if it were yesterday. I know the date because it's written in my Bible beside Habakkuk 3:17-19. I took this beautiful proclamation of faith and made it my own. Like Habakkuk, I was quaking in my boots. I felt sick to my stomach as I wrote:

- *Though* I never understand *Why*,
- *though* I never see my daughter smile again,
- *though* she makes wrong choices,
- *though* this pain in my heart never goes away.

Yet will I exult in the Lord. I will rejoice in the God of my salvation. The Lord God is my strength, and He has made my feet like hinds' feet, and makes me walk on my high places.

The decision to choose to trust in the dark was the beginning of my healing. My eyes shifted from circumstances to the Sovereign Lord who was still the Blessed Controller of all things.

YET WILL YOU TRUST HIM?

Life has times of prosperity and times of adversity, the straight and the crooked. When your heart is breaking with a burden, do you wait on God? Have you seen Him in all His majesty, and can you say with Habakkuk that the righteous shall live by faith? We all need a faith that perseveres through the times when we can't see what God is doing but we can see *Him*, and so we say, "Yet will I trust You."

I don't know your Thoughs: *Though* my parents never understand or support me . . . *Though* I never have a husband . . . *Though* my husband disappoints me . . . *Though* I'm exhausted . . . *Though* I am in pain . . . *Though* my child turns away from Christ.

Though, though, though . . . YET WILL I TRUST THE LORD GOD. HE IS MY STRENGTH.

A Personal

Letter

A Personal Letter

My Dear Friend,

    I feel like you've become my friend. We've been taking a journey together. I've been sharing with you what I'm learning and where God is taking me. I pray you are encouraged to go forward on your own journey to contentment!

    This morning I revisited Psalm 84. It has long been a favorite of mine. As I read it again, I was reminded of the journey to calmness of heart. It speaks of a woman like you and me who sets her heart on pilgrimage. A *pilgrim* is defined as "a person who travels to a sacred place." Contentment is a holy place. According to this psalm, the woman is blessed because her strength is in God. As she travels through the valley of weeping, she makes it into a living spring (verses 5-6). My prayer is that you, too, will reach the living spring of contentment.

    My personal journey has been a pilgrimage of yielding control of my circumstances to God. In order for God to show me how He is the Blessed Controller in my life, He had to chip away at my masterful methods of control. It was as if I were sitting in the back seat of a Land Rover in a little car seat that had its own steering wheel. I was turning the wheel left, then right, but I never realized that my steering wheel wasn't connected to anything. One day I looked up and realized that I wasn't the one driving.

    I finally saw that although I have a steering wheel, I can give up control. My Driver (God) is totally in control. He has been on the road. He knows the way. He sees ahead to the very end of the road — to all my tomorrows. I can sit back and relax, converse with the Driver, and enjoy the journey. My focus becomes *Him* instead of where I'm going.

To be honest, at the beginning of my pilgrimage I thought my secret choices of obedience would someday bring me to the place where I could declare with Paul, "I have learned to be content whatever the circumstances" (Philippians 4:11). I know now that choices made deep in my heart, secretly between me and my God, *are* a significant part of contentment. However, twenty years into my journey to a calm heart, it's very clear to me that Paul spoke truth when he said the key to contentment was this: "I have strength for all things in Christ Who empowers me — I am ready for anything and equal to anything through Him Who infuses inner strength into me" (Philippians 4:13, AMP).

What I have been sharing with you throughout this book is that first, foremost, and finally, *contentment is a yielding to our Great, Almighty, Holy King.* "God . . . is the blessed controller of all things, the king over all kings and the master of all masters" (1 Timothy 6:15, PH). He is the Blessed Controller of our circumstances, gifts, abilities, possessions, roles, and relationships. We acknowledge His sovereign control by trusting Him for everything: what we don't understand, what we can't see, and what doesn't make sense to us. When God becomes our total trust, we humbly accept our portion and our cup (Psalm 16:5). We accept what He has allowed in the past. We accept what He has allowed today. And we give all our tomorrows to Him. A humility grows within us that He is the loving controller of *all* life.

As we grow in trusting God in all things, our contentment becomes an act of worship. Isn't that a beautiful thought! One of my favorite old writers said that we worship God more by contentment than when we come to hear a sermon or spend a half-hour in prayer. These are certainly acts of worshiping God, but they are only external.[1] The soul worship of God is to be content with what He gives, to be thankful in all things. When we humbly yield to God's plan and purpose for our lives, it is an act of worship. I love thinking that my life can literally bring worship to Him.

When we've given all our questions to God, when we're not

grumbling about the past or anxious about the future, when our tomorrows are in His keeping, we are free to wake up every morning and say, "God, You've given me today as a gift. Show me how to glorify You in it."

Peace wraps around your heart when you're able to trust God for just today and not be burdened with the *If Onlys*, the *What Ifs*, and the *Whys*. The questions are for His safekeeping. The tomorrows are His, and you are free! You are free because God Himself has become your sufficiency. He is your contentment. What does your freedom produce? An ability to concentrate on others and their needs, to encourage others, to love and serve the people God brings into your life. You can reach out because God has reached inside you.

Picture in your mind a woman who is content. Perhaps you know such a woman. What does she possess? You might list the fruit of the Spirit: love, joy, peace, patience, and all the rest. What doesn't she possess? An anxious heart. The crown called contentment is not on her head but in her heart. Her contentment doesn't depend on people, places, or possessions. This is who you and I long to become. We know such a woman is a rare jewel.

I love this story that illustrates such contentment.

> A king was suffering from a painful ailment and was told that the only cure for him was to find a contented man, get his shirt, and wear it night and day. So messengers were sent through the king's realm in search of such a man, with orders to bring back his shirt. Months passed. After a thorough search of the country, the messengers returned without the shirt.
>
> "Did you find a contented man in all my realm?" the king asked.
>
> "Yes, O King, we found one, just one in all the realm."

"Then why did you not bring back his shirt?"
the king demanded.

"Master, the man had no shirt."[2]

Together we've been journeying toward becoming that rare woman who is content in all things (with or without a shirt!). My prayer for you, my friend, and for me, is that we become women whose hearts are calm and trusting, able to say:

> *The Lord is my peace. I shall not live in anxiety. He puts me under His wing of comfort and calms my spirit within me. He takes all my anxieties on Himself and helps me to focus on Him. Yes, though I walk through a time of grave uncertainties and fierce anxieties, I will not fret — for You are my peace. Your Word and Your presence calm me now. You hold my uncertainties in the palm of Your hand. You, soothe my anxious mind — You smooth my wrinkled brow. Surely serenity and trust in You shall fill me all the days of my life. And I shall keep my mind stayed on You forever.*[3]

Twelve-Week

Bible Study

for

—

Calm
My Anxious
Heart

Twelve-Week Bible Study for
Calm My Anxious Heart

Dear Friend,

I'm excited about what God is going to do in your life as a result of your choice to do this study! I pray that God will calm your anxious heart and reveal more of Himself to you as you study His Word.

Bible study is good, but *memorizing* and *meditating* on God's Word are the best ways to place His Word in your heart and mind. Cynthia Heald said that memorizing Scripture increases the Holy Spirit's vocabulary in your life.[1] For this reason, each of these twelve lessons includes verses to memorize. Only as we lay up God's Word and wisdom in our hearts will we be changed.

If you're like me, you have good intentions to memorize God's Word, but without accountability your intentions quickly fizzle out. Memorization is never easy, but you will be grateful you did it when you see the difference it makes in your daily life. If the memorization assignment seems too long, pick one verse and learn it well. Then use your verse (or verses) to praise God and pray your verses back to Him. Here's an example of how you might do that with the verses from the first week's study.

> *Verses*: Philippians 4:11-13: "For I have learned to
> be content whatever the circumstances. I know
> what it is to be in need, and I know what it is to
> have plenty. I have learned the secret of being
> content in any and every situation, whether
> well fed or hungry, whether living in plenty or

in want. I can do everything through him who
gives me strength."

My Praise: God, I thank you for Paul's example.
His words overwhelm me. I give You praise that
Paul says he learned to be content. That means
I, too, can learn! I praise You that Paul's secret
of contentment is clear — his dependent trust in
God who gave him the strength to be content in
all circumstances.

My Prayer: Oh, God, how far short I fall of Paul's
words. But Lord, my desire is to learn to be
content. I long to have You calm my anxious
heart, to enable me to say with Paul, "I have
learned to be content in all circumstances." I
know that growing to depend on You is the key;
teach me how to do this.

In this example I have written my praise and prayer sepa-
rately, but when I memorize Scripture and pray it back to God in
the form of a request or praise, I usually combine the two.

It is such a joy to store up God's Word in your heart and then
talk to Him about it! I encourage you to do this weekly as you
memorize Scripture. It will give you a practical way to meditate on
God's wonderful Word.

Memorizing Scripture is one important part of this Bible
study. Another important part is writing in your *My Journey to
Contentment* journal. This is a record of what God is teaching you
so that you will remember what He's done for you in the past when
present circumstances are difficult.

When the Israelites crossed the Red Sea on dry ground,
God instructed them to "take up twelve stones from the middle
of the Jordan ... to serve as a sign among you ... a memorial"

(Joshua 4:3,6,7). We can easily forget God's goodness when times are tough. That's why we need memorials to prompt our minds and spirits to remembrance. Your journal is your "twelve stones."

A matching companion journal has been specifically designed to help you personalize the Scripture memory and record God's goodness; the twelve sections correlate with each chapter and Bible study in *Calm My Anxious Heart*.

Each week, write your answers to the following questions in your journal and then write a prayer in response: (1) What did I learn about God this week? (2) What did I learn about myself this week? (3) Write a prayer to "remember" what God has taught you.

My prayer for you is that six months or five years from now you will return to your journal and read and rejoice over what God has taught you. God is your teacher. May He show you much about His mercies, His love, and what it truly means to be content in all circumstances.

I will be praying for you as you learn from Him.

Linda Dillow

WEEK 1

Read chapter 1, "My Journey to Contentment."

1. Memorize Philippians 4:11-13. Write the verses on a card and go over them every day. Pray the verses back to God and ask Him to burn His truth into your heart.

2. Write a paraphrase of Philippians 4:11-13.

3. Meditate on Philippians 4:11-13 and what you have read in chapter 1 of *Calm My Anxious Heart*. (To meditate means "to think about or consider, to give up oneself to serious thought.") Then write a definition of *contentment*.

4. Write out Ella Spees' five statements that made up her prescription for contentment. See page 13.

5. How do you think Ella Spees' was able to have a "holy
    habit" of contentment? Refer to page 13.

6. Read 1 Timothy 6:15, NASB. Look up the word *sovereign*
    in the dictionary or a Bible dictionary. Write a
    paraphrase of the verse using what you learn about this
    word.

7. What difference would it make if you truly let God be
    the Blessed Controller of your circumstances? Give a
    practical example.

8. Reread the story of the two monks on page 19.

    a. Which monk do you think describes you?

    b. Do you think most women try to control or manipulate people and circumstances? If yes, why?

9. Write in your journal: (1) What did I learn about God this week? (2) What did I learn about myself? (3) Write a prayer to remember what God has taught you.

WEEK 2

Read chapter 2, "Content with Circumstances."

1. Memorize Philippians 4:6-8. Write the verses on a card and go over them every day. Pray and praise God, using your memory verses.

2. Refer to page 28 in chapter 2 and write lists of the positive and negative aspects of the circumstances God has allowed in your life at this time.

   a. Positives

   b. Negatives

3. Which list do you dwell on most? What has God shown you through this exercise?

4. Look at your negative list (question 2b). Choose the most troubling circumstance on this list and write it here.

5. According to Philippians 4:6, what two choices are you to make concerning this difficult circumstance in your life?

6. Meditate on Philippians 4:7. How do you define peace? What do you think it will feel like when you possess it?

7. Meditate on Philippians 4:8. What is your part? Write out specifically what this means in the midst of your circumstance.

8. In Philippians 4:9, we are instructed to practice "these things."

   a. What things are we to practice? Refer to page 33 and to Philippians 4:6-9.

   b. List three ways you can practice "these things" this week.

9. Are you in the process of learning to be content with your circumstances? Give a practical example from your life of how you see yourself moving toward contentment.

10. Write in your journal, *My Journey to Contentment*: (1) What did I learn about God this week? (2) What did I learn about myself? (3) Write a prayer to remember what God has taught you.

WEEK 3

Read chapter 3, "Content to Be Me."

    1. Memorize Psalm 139:14.

    2. Each day this week read Psalm 139:13-16 out loud. Then pray it back to God. What new insights has God shown you from this psalm?

    3. Paraphrase Psalm 139:13-16.

    4. Are you willing to be stretched to discover your abilities and spiritual gifts?

    5. List your abilities. Be honest and specific. How are you using your talents to glorify God?

6. Look up the word *character* in the dictionary. Write the definition below. Have you focused on developing your character or have you been focused on activities? Give an example from your life.

7. What is your attitude about your personality? Your body? Your abilities? Do you think your attitude pleases God?

8. Your Physical Appearance

   a. What do you need to accept and thank God for concerning your physical appearance?

   b. Is there anything you need to do to better maintain the body God has given you?

9. a. List two of your character traits that you believe
       please God.

   b. List two of your character traits that you believe
       displease God. Pick one and ask God to show you
       His plan for working on this trait this week. Write
       your plan here.

10. What difference would it make in your life and
    relationships if you accepted and lived God's truth in
    Psalm 139?

11. Of the women you know, whom do you consider to be
    a Proverbs 31 woman? Interview her this week and ask
    her how she became a woman of character.

12. Write in your journal: (1) What did I learn about God
    this week? (2) What did I learn about myself? (3)
    Write a prayer to remember what God has taught you.

WEEK 4

Read chapter 4, "Content with My Role."

1. Memorize Matthew 20:28. Write it on a card and carry it with you. As you learn it, pray the verse back to God.

2. Listed below are eight ways to guarantee that you will become discontent in your roles. Identify the scriptural antidote for each discontent by using your memory verses, Philippians 4:11-13, Philippians 4:6-9, Psalm 139:14, and Matthew 20:28. The first one (2a) is completed for you.

    a. Refuse to accept what God has given.
       Philippians 4:11: Contentment is found in accepting whatever circumstances God allows in my life. "Oh, God, help me to remember this on a daily basis and truly live it."
    b. Dwell on the negative in your husband, children, roommate, or colleague.
    c. Look for contentment everywhere but in God.
    d. Carry all your anxieties yourself.
    e. Count your problems instead of your blessings.
    f. Pray only about the things you can't handle yourself.
    g. Make grumbling a habit.
    h. Doubt God's love and sovereign control in your life.

3. Do you find yourself wishing you could trade places with someone? Considering what God has said about you in Psalm 139, how do you think God would feel about you comparing yourself and your life to those of other women?

4. a. If you are married, list five excellent and praiseworthy qualities about your husband. If you are single, list the excellent qualities of the most important person in your life.

   b. Write a letter or note to your husband (or the person you chose under 4a), describing the qualities you appreciate in him or her.

5. God's standard for us as Christians is faithfulness (1 Corinthians 4:2). What does it mean, practically speaking, for you to be faithful in your roles?

6. How can you apply Matthew 20:28 and serve the people in your life this week? Write in the space below what you think God would have you do.

7. Write in your journal: (1) What did I learn about God this week? (2) What did I learn about myself? (3) Write a prayer to remember what God has taught you.

WEEK 5

Read chapter 5, "Content in Relationships."

1. Memorize Colossians 3:12-14.

2. Has someone offended you? Picture in your mind any individuals who cause you to feel frustration, anger, or sorrow. Write their names and the reason for your hurt in the space below.

3. Have you offended someone? Write the name or names and why they are upset.

4. Forgiveness is difficult! Mark any of the following statements you've found yourself thinking.

   > I'll forgive, but I won't forget.
   > If I forgive now, this person will get off too easily. She (or he) should pay for the offense.
   > Why do I always have to be the one to do the right thing?
   > Why should I forgive? This person isn't even sorry for what happened.

* I can forgive this person for what she did to me, but not for the pain she (or he) has caused others.
* I'm not sure that forgiving this person is necessary. After all, I don't hate him (or her), I'd just rather avoid situations where we come in contact.
* I've tried to forgive this person, but he (or she) keeps doing the same things over and over.

5. Review Matthew 18:21-35. Listed below are God's attitudes toward you as pictured in this passage. Based upon His attitudes, write the corresponding attitude you should have toward the individuals you listed in question 2 of this week's study. The first example is done for you.

God's Attitude Toward Me	My Attitude Toward Others
Has forgiven me everything.	*I need to forgive (fill in name).*
Forgave me even though I didn't deserve it.	
Forgives me over and over for the same sin.	
Forgives even my most horrific offenses.	
Forgives me quickly, never holding a grudge.	

6. Pray the following prayer:
   God, You are so good. Your grace is beyond my comprehension. Your mercies are new every morning. How quick I am to disappoint You; how quick You are to forgive me. Thank You,

*Jesus, for all You suffered because of what I've done. May I
never take Your death upon the cross for granted.*

7. Now pray the following prayer for each person you
    listed in question 2:
    *God, You know how (name) has hurt me by (state the offense).
    In the name of Jesus, who has forgiven me everything, I now
    choose to forgive this person. I lay (name) at Your feet and all
    the pain I've experienced because of what's happened. I ask now
    for You to begin Your healing work in my heart and in our
    relationship.*

8. Read Colossians 3:12-15 and Romans 15:5-7. In
    column 1, list any key words or phrases Paul uses to
    communicate the idea of unity in the body of Christ.
    In column 2, list the actions or attitudes that can help
    maintain that unity.

WORDS OR PHRASES THAT SUGGEST UNITY	HOW WE CAN MAINTAIN UNITY

9. What does it mean to go beyond forgiveness? How did
    Jesus go beyond forgiveness with those who crucified
    Him? (Luke 23:34); with Judas? (Matthew 26:50); with
    Peter? (Mark 16:6-7).

10. Make a list of several people you have had to forgive in the past. Thank God for the work He has done. Now ask Him, "Is there anything further You want me to do to extend love and grace toward this person?" Write down anything you think you should do.

11. Write Colossians 3:12-14 from memory, inserting the name of the person you need to forgive and love.

12. Write in your journal: (1) What did I learn about God this week? (2) What did I learn about myself? (3) Write a prayer to remember what God has taught you.

WEEK 6

Read chapter 6, "Never Enough."

1. Memorize and meditate on Hebrews 13:5 and Psalm 119:14. Write the verses on a card and go over them every day.

2. Everything belongs to God. Read 1 Chronicles 29:11-14. Write a paragraph expressing what it means to you personally that "everything is the Lord's."

3. Greed is an issue of the heart. What practical ways can you apply Psalm 62:10? How can you keep your heart in the right place (Matthew 6:19-21)?

4. God comes first, possessions second. What does it mean to you to love money (1 Timothy 6:10)? Read Hebrews 13:5 and list ways you can keep your life free from the love of money.

5. Possessions are to be used, not loved. Read Proverbs
   30:8-9. What made Agur's attitude so pure? Do you
   think you possess this same spirit toward possessions?

6. Ask yourself these hard questions about money and
   possessions: (a) What is God's standard for Christians
   concerning these two things? (b) Should my standard
   of living increase if my income increases? (c) How
   much money should I give to the Lord's work? What
   are your answers?

7. Pick one thing from the section entitled "What Can
   You Do at Your House?" (pages 97–101), and write a
   paragraph outlining how you will "Search Your Heart,"
   "Cut the Ropes," "Submit to Plastic Surgery," or "Share
   Your Wealth."

8. Read and meditate on 1 Timothy 6:6-19. Then answer these questions.

  a. Find all of the statements in these verses about money, riches, and those who are rich. Rephrase the statements in your own words.

  b. In verse 11, Timothy is instructed to "flee from all this." From what is he instructed to flee (verse 10)? How do we flee? Give a practical example of how you have done this.

  c. What instructions are given us in verses 12 and 17-19? What does this mean to you this week? How can you do this?

9. What steps can you take to combat "seasonal overspending"? List at least three things.

10. Write in your journal: (1) What did I learn about God this week? (2) What did I learn about myself? (3) Write a prayer to remember what God has taught you.

WEEK 7

Read chapter 7, "A Faulty Focus." This week's lesson is a little different from the other studies. The goal is to encourage you to discover your life purpose statement. You will be asked to share your thoughts with the group. It should be an exciting study!

1. Memorize Ephesians 5:15-17. You can memorize from your Bible or the Phillips translation (page 110).

2. List at least five benefits of developing a life purpose statement.

3. How did you feel when you read the life purpose statements of Phyllis, Jean, Ney, and Mimi? Hopeful? Motivated? Ready to write your life purpose? Or did you feel discouraged? Explain.

4. Read the chapter a second time and ask God to begin to reveal to you what your life purpose statement is. (Remember: You don't have to be clever or creative.)

5. If you have a life verse, write it down. If not, write down verses that God has used in your life.

6. Spend an hour alone with God. Ask Him to reveal His life purpose statement for you. Write down any thoughts or ideas that come to you during this time. (Remember: You can take ideas from Phyllis, Jean, Ney, and Mimi. They've given their permission.)

7. Write in your journal: (1) What have I learned about God this week? (2) What have I learned about myself? (3) Write a prayer to remember what God has taught you.

WEEK 8

Read chapter 8, "Worry Is Like a Rocking Chair."

  1. Memorize 1 Peter 5:6-7.

  2. Look up the words *worry* and *anxiety* in a dictionary or
     Bible dictionary. Refer to the definitions on page 127
     and then write your own definitions.

  3. Read Matthew 6:25-34.

     a. What is the opposite of worry in verse 30?

     b. What do you think the word *therefore* in verse 34
        means?

     c. Why did Jesus tell the disciples five times not to
        worry?

The next question is designed to help you consider what causes
you anxiety — why you worry and when you worry. The following
three examples are to get you going!

WHAT	WHY	WHEN
The house payment	Not enough money	When I see the balance in my checkbook
The way I look in my clothes	I've gained ten pounds, clothes are tight	When I have to change out of my sweats
Cancer	Lump in my breast	Twenty-four hours a day

4. Fill out the following chart, showing what you worry about, why, and when.

WHAT	WHY	WHEN

5. Pray that God helps you to make WAR on worry. W stands for *what*, A stands for *action*, and R for *relinquishment*. Write down each item under the *What* column on your chart. If there is an action God would have you take, list it. If the worry is something out of your control, relinquish it to God by casting it on His strong shoulders. Three examples are provided for you.

a. Worry: the house payment. Action: I can call the bank and see if it's possible to get a loan. Or we could take the vacation money, make the payment, and not have a vacation this year.

b. Worry: the way I look in my clothes. Action: I can buy some new clothes or lose ten pounds.

c. Worry: I might have cancer. Relinquishment: "Lord, You know my anguish over this lump. I can't handle it. I humble myself under Your mighty hand and cast this anxiety on You."

6. Look up the word *humble* in a dictionary or Bible dictionary. Write a paragraph describing what it means to you to humble yourself under "God's mighty hand" (1 Peter 5:6).

7. How can you "cast your anxieties on the Lord"? Would the anxiety box described on pages 134–135 or another visual aid help you?

8. *A Memory Test.* What were you worrying about this time last year? Do you think you would handle the situation differently now? How?

9. Write in your journal: (1) What did I learn about God this week? (2) What did I learn about myself? (3) Write a prayer to remember what God has taught you.

WEEK 9

Read chapter 9, "Faith: The Foundation."

    1. Memorize Hebrews 11:1.

    2. How do you define faith? Write your definition here.

    3. Read Genesis 15:1-5. What did God promise Abraham and Sarah? What was Abraham's response in verse 6?

    4. In the book of Genesis, we see Sarah's journey of faith, her victories, and her defeats. Read Genesis 16:1-6. In this passage we see that Sarah's eyes have shifted from faith in God's Word to what she can see and feel.

      a. Describe how Sarah took control and manipulated the circumstances.

b. What relationships were harmed because of her actions?

5. How did Sarah fail once again to trust God in Genesis 18:1-15?

6. Genesis 21:1-7 reveals God's faithfulness to Sarah in spite of her failures to trust Him. Describe the "Sarah of faith" seen here.

7. We also see the mature Sarah in Hebrews 11:11 and 1 Peter 3:5-6. What do these verses tell you about Sarah's trust in God?

8. When Sarah couldn't see what God was doing, she found it difficult to wait for God's time schedule. Perhaps you can't see what God is doing in your life today. Reread pages 143–145 about our faith being rooted in God's character. What aspect of God's character is mentioned in Hebrews 10:23 and Hebrews 11:11? How can this attribute of God's be an encouragement to you?

9. Read Proverbs 3:5,6. What is God's command to you when you're tempted to take control?

10. Think of a difficult situation in your life right now. Will you pray and allow God to be the Blessed Controller of your difficulty? Write a prayer in the space below, telling God that you want to focus your eyes on His character and that you want to live, not by your feelings, but "by faith."

11. Write in your journal: (1) What did I learn about God this week? (2) What did I learn about myself? (3) Write a prayer to remember what God has taught you.

WEEK 10

Read chapter 10, "Trusting God with the *What Ifs*." The spiritual disease of asking, "*What If?*" is deadly. *What If* looks to the future and worries about what God might allow. A symptom of this disease is an anxious heart.

1. Memorize Jeremiah 17:7-8. Make these verses your prayer.

2. What are your *What Ifs?* What do you fear God might allow in your life or the lives of those you love? List your fears in the space below.

3. Identify a time when you were anxious about something that might happen — a time when you had the *What If* disease. What happened in your body, mind, and spirit?

4. Read Jeremiah 17:5-8. Write a paraphrase of these verses.

5. How do control, strategies, intelligence, and manipulation keep you from becoming a woman whose trust is in the Lord?

6. Ask yourself this question: "Am I going to judge God by the circumstances I don't understand or judge the circumstances in light of the character of God?" What would help you to view your life in light of the character of God?

7. Read the story of Moses' mother, Jochebed, in Exodus 2:1-10 and answer these questions:

   a. What were Jochebed's *What Ifs?*

   b. How did she deal with her *What Ifs?*

8. Look at Willis Carrier's three-step plan for handling worry on page 163. Write your worst *What If* in the space below and work through the three steps.

9. Write a prayer of relinquishment, giving your worst
   What If to God.

10. Write in your journal: (1) What did I learn about God
    this week? (2) What did I learn about myself? (3)
    Write a prayer to remember what God has taught you.

WEEK 11

Read chapter 11, "Trusting God with the *If Onlys.*" The spiritual disease "*If Only*" is also deadly. *If Only* looks to the past and grumbles over what God has given. Anger and complaining are symptoms of this disease.

1. Memorize Psalm 77:11-14.

2. Reread the story about the old man and the white horse on pages 171–173. Share the story with someone in your family or with a friend. Tell the person what you have learned from the story. Write what you have learned in the space below.

3. We catch the *If Only* disease when we dwell on what we don't have instead of on what we *do* have. The *If Only* disease is caused by discontent with what God has given.

   a. Write a list of the *If Onlys* that attack you.

b. When you dwell on the *If Onlys*, do you lose
    perspective as the Israelites did? How does this
    show itself in your life?

4. Read the story of Lazarus's death in John 11. Jesus
    wants to meet your *If* with His *If*, as He did for Martha.
    What does that mean to you?

5. Read Numbers 20:1-5. In this passage, the people
    complained to their leaders, but they were really angry
    at God. This is called "displaced anger." Describe a
    time when you displaced your anger on someone.

6. The way to survive the packages of pain God allows in
    your life is to remember who God is and what He has
    done in the past for you. Read Psalm 77 at least twice.
    Remember the deeds of the Lord and list them in the
    space below.

7. Reread Andrew Murray's four-step encouragement
   for trusting God in the midst of trouble (see page 181).
   Identify the trouble that is causing you to contract the
   If Only disease. Using your problem, write out the four
   steps.

8. Will you write a prayer confessing to God that you have
   not trusted Him when you have dwelled on the *If Onlys?*

9. Write in your journal: (1) What did I learn about God
   this week? (2) What did I learn about myself? (3)
   Write a prayer to remember what God has taught you.

WEEK 12

Read chapter 12, "Trusting God with the *Whys*."

1. Memorize Habakkuk 3:17-19.

2. Describe a time when you asked God, "Why me?"
    Were you able to move from asking why to trusting in
    God?

3. How would you explain Ecclesiastes 7:13-14 to a child?
    Write your explanation in the space below.

4. Set aside an hour to read Habakkuk 1:1–2:4 and 3:16-19
    and answer the following questions. Ask God to speak
    to you through this faithful prophet.

    a. Every one of us has problems that cause heartache,
        fear, frustration, and a lack of contentment. Write
        out a description to God of a problem that is heavy
        on your heart.

b. Station yourself "on the ramparts." Ask God to
    speak to you concerning your problem. Be still
    before God. Then write down your thoughts.

c. According to Romans 11:36, what is the ultimate
    purpose of all things? In what ways do you think
    your present circumstances bring glory to God?

d. How can God's answer to Habakkuk, "The just
    shall live by faith," be an answer for you concerning
    your problem?

e. Will you trust God for what you can't see, what you don't understand, and what doesn't make sense to you? Will you list your *Thoughs* to God?

❧ Though

❧ Though

❧ Though

❧ Though

❧ Though

If you can, say with Habakkuk, "Yet I will rejoice in the LORD, I will be joyful in God my Savior. *The Sovereign LORD Is My Strength!*" (Habbakuk 3:18-19, capitalization and emphasis mine).

5. Write in your journal: (1) What did I learn about God this week? (2) What did I learn about myself? (3) Write a prayer to remember what God has taught you.

Notes

Chapter 1: My Journey to Contentment

1. Mary W. Tileston, *Daily Strength for Daily Needs* (London: Messrs. Samson, Lowe and Co., 1928), p. 144. Ella Spees' adapted her habits of contentment from a selection by E. B. Pusey (1800–1882) in this book by Mary.

2. Paul Lee Tan, *Encyclopedia of 7700 Illustrations* (Rockville, MD: Assurance Publishers, 1979), pp. 272–273.

3. Charles D. Kelley, "The Miracle of Contentment," *Discipleship Journal* (November/December 1987), p. 32.

4. Kenneth Wuest, *Philippians in the Greek New Testament* (Grand Rapids: Eerdmans, 1948), p. 114.

5. J. I. Packer, "The Secret of Contentment," address given at Wheaton College, Wheaton, IL, 27 February 1984.

6. Elisabeth Elliot, *The Elisabeth Elliot Newsletter* (March-April 1995), p. 1.

7. Mrs. Charles E. Cowman, *Streams in the Desert* (Grand Rapids: Zondervan, 1925), p. 108.

Chapter 2: Content with Circumstances

1. Adapted from Linda Dillow, *How to Really Love Your Man* (Nashville: Nelson, 1993), p. 131.

Chapter 3: Content to Be Me

1. For a good discussion of this psalm, see John F. Walvoord and Roy B. Zuck, *The Bible Knowledge Commentary* (Wheaton, IL: Victor, 1985) and C. H. Spurgeon, *The Treasury of David*, vol. 3 (Grand Rapids: Zondervan, 1966), p. 262.

2. James Hufstetler, "On Knowing Oneself," *The Banner of Truth* 280 (January 1987), p. 13.

3. Quoted by J. R. Miller in a printed message, "Finding One's Mission" (Swengel, PA: Peiner Publications, n.d.), p. 2.

4. Jerry Bridges, *Trusting God Even When It Hurts* (Colorado Springs, CO: NavPress, 1988), pp. 165–166.

5. Bridges, p. 166.

6. Edythe Draper, *Draper's Book of Quotations for the Christian World* (Wheaton, IL: Tyndale, 1992), p. 1825.

7. Adapted from an allegory by Mrs. Charles E. Cowman, *Streams in the Desert* (Grand Rapids: Zondervan, 1925), p. 271.

8. George MacDonald, *Unspoken Sermons, Series Three* (London: Longmans, Green, and Co., 1981), p. 6.

9. Barbara K. Mouser, *Five Aspects of Woman* (Mountlake Terrace, WA: WinePress Publishing, 1992), p. 15.

10. Mrs. Charles E. Cowman, *Streams in the Desert,* vol. 2 (Grand Rapids: Zondervan, 1966), p. 235.

CHAPTER 4: CONTENT WITH MY ROLE

1. This e-mail sketch is adapted from an original work written by Leola Floren, Michigan-based newspaper columnist and author of *The New Boss Has a Milk Mustache* (Kansas City, MO: Beacon Hill Press, 1996). Used by permission.

2. Elisabeth Elliot, *Loneliness* (Nashville: Nelson, 1988), pp. 33–39.

3. Elliot, pp. 40–41.

4. Dr. Larry Crabb, *The Marriage Builder* (Grand Rapids: Zondervan, 1982), p. 50.

CHAPTER 5: CONTENT IN RELATIONSHIPS

1. *USA Today,* 6 January 1977, p. 1.

2. Charles R. Swindoll, *Growing Strong in the Seasons of Life* (Portland, OR: Multnomah, 1983), p. 248.

3. Swindoll, p. 249.

4. Philip Yancey, "An Unnatural Act," *Christianity Today* (8 April 1991), p. 39.
5. Yancey, p. 36.
6. Clara Barton, cited by Luis Palau in the message "Experiencing God's Forgiveness."

CHAPTER 6: NEVER ENOUGH

1. Richard Swenson, MD, *Margin* (Colorado Springs, CO: NavPress, 1992), p. 164.
2. *USA Today*, 22 November 1996, sec. A, p. 8.
3. Interview with Dave Ramsey, *People* 17 February 1997, pp. 69–70.
4. Ramsey, *People*.
5. Colin Greer, "Interview with Billy Graham," *People* (20 October 1996), p. 5.
6. A. W. Tozer, *The Pursuit of God* (Harrisburg, PA: Christian Publications, 1948), p. 22.
7. *Colorado Springs Gazette Telegraph*, 25 November 1996, sec. D, p. 1.
8. Angel Tree is Chuck Colson's gift-giving ministry to the children of prisoners.
9. Michael P. Green, *Illustrations for Biblical Preaching* (Grand Rapids: Baker, 1982), p. 121.

CHAPTER 7: A FAULTY FOCUS

1. Richard Swenson, MD, *Margin* (Colorado Springs, CO: NavPress, 1992), p. 157.
2. Message by Phyllis Stanley, "Living Purposely," Colorado Springs, CO, 1997.
3. Message by Dr. Charles R. Swindoll, "Who Gets the Glory?" Northwest Bible Church, Dallas, TX.
4. Iain H. Murray, *Jonathan Edwards: A New Biography* (Carlisle, PA.: Banner of Truth Trust, 1987), pp. 42–44. He made seventy such resolutions!

5. Elisabeth Elliot, *Let Me Be a Woman* (Wheaton, IL: Tyndale, 1976), p. 10.
6. Personal interview with Phyllis Stanley.
7. Jean Fleming, *Finding Focus in a Whirlwind World* (Fort Collins, CO: Treasure, 1991), p. 37.
8. Personal interview with Jean Fleming. Also, *Finding Focus in a Whirlwind World*, pp. 40–42.
9. Personal interview with Ney Bailey.
10. Ney Bailey heard this prayer given by Elisabeth Elliot.
11. Personal interview with Mimi Wilson.
12. Ron Mehl, "A Place of Quiet Rest," *Discipleship Journal* (May/June 1997), p. 24.

CHAPTER 8: WORRY IS LIKE A ROCKING CHAIR

1. Mrs. Charles E. Cowman, *Streams in the Desert* (Grand Rapids: Zondervan, 1925), p. 118.
2. Frank Minirth, MD, Paul Meier, MD, and Don Hawkins, ThM, *Worry-Free Living* (Nashville: Thomas Nelson, 1989), p. 17.
3. Minirth., p. 28.
4. Paul Lee Tan, *Encyclopedia of 7700 Illustrations* (Rockville, MD, Meier, Hawkins: Assurance Publishers, 1997), p. 1648.
5. Kenneth Wuest, *Word Studies in the Greek New Testament* (Grand Rapids: Eerdmans, 1980), vol. 1.
6. Bishop Fulton J. Sheen, quoted by Frank S. Mead, *12,000 Religious Quotations* (Grand Rapids: Baker, 1989), p. 478.
7. Oswald Chambers, May 23 entry, *My Utmost for His Highest* (New York: Dodd, Mead & Co., 1935).
8. George MacDonald, *Annals of a Quiet Neighborhood* (Philadelphia: David McKay, n.d.), p. 203.
9. Mrs. Charles E. Cowman, *Streams in the Desert* (Grand Rapids: Zondervan, 1925), p. 23.
10. James Montgomery Boice, *The Sermon on the Mount* (Grand Rapids: Zondervan, 1972), p. 257.

CHAPTER 9: FAITH: THE FOUNDATION

1. Amy Carmichael, *You Are My Hiding Place: Devotional Readings Arranged by David Hazard* (Minneapolis: Bethany House, 1991), p. 10.
2. Ney Bailey, *Faith Is Not a Feeling* (Orlando, FL: Campus Crusade for Christ, 1979), p. 23.
3. Oswald Chambers, May 8 entry, *My Utmost for His Highest* (New York: Dodd, Mead & Co., 1935).
4. Mrs. Charles Cowman, *Streams in the Desert* (Grand Rapids: Zondervan, 1925), p. 180.
5. Cowman, pp. 377–378.

CHAPTER 10: TRUSTING GOD WITH THE *WHAT IFS*

1. Eugenia Semyonovna Ginsburg, *Journey into the Whirlwind* (New York: Harcourt Brace, 1975), p. 16.
2. Bill Hull, *Anxious for Nothing* (Old Tappan, NJ: Revell, 1987), pp. 86–87.
3. H. E. Manning, quoted by Elisabeth Elliot, *Keep a Quiet Heart* (Ann Arbor, MI: Servant, 1995), p. 147.
4. Dale Carnegie, *How to Stop Worrying and Start Living* (New York: Simon & Schuster, 1944), pp. 16–23.
5. Reinhold Niebuhr quoted in *Ageless Inspirations* compiled by Ellie Busha (Ventura, CA: Evergreen Communications, Inc., 1990), p. 31.

CHAPTER 11: TRUSTING GOD WITH THE *IF ONLYS*

1. Translated from the Portuguese, Max Lucado, *In the Eye of the Storm* (Dallas: Word, 1991), pp. 144–147.
2. Isobel Kuhn, *Green Leaf in Drought* (OMF Books, 1958), pp. 40–42.
3. Michael P. Green, *Illustrations for Biblical Preaching* (Grand Rapids: Baker, 1982), p. 388.

CHAPTER 12: TRUSTING GOD WITH THE *WHYS*

1. Myrna Alexander, *Behold Your God: A Woman's Workshop on the Attributes of God* (Grand Rapids: Zondervan, 1978), p. 29.
2. J. Sidlow Baxter, *Explore the Book*, vol. 4 (Grand Rapids: Zondervan, 1964), p. 212.

A PERSONAL LETTER

1. Jeremiah Burroughs, *The Rare Jewel of Christian Contentment* (Carlisle, PA: The Banner of Truth Trust, 1979), p. 23.
2. Paul Lee Tan, *Encyclopedia of 7700 Illustrations* (Rockville, MD: Assurance Publishers, 1979), pp. 272–273.
3. A paraphrase of Psalm 23, written by my friend Judy Booth.

TWELVE-WEEK BIBLE STUDY

1. From a message given at a Tri-Lakes Chapel, Women's Retreat, Monument, CO, April 1995.

Author

LINDA DILLOW and her husband, Jody, have lived in Europe and Asia and have been involved in international ministry for twenty-five years. Linda speaks at women's retreats and conferences in America, Asia, and Europe.

Her books include *A Deeper Kind of Calm*, *Satisfy My Thirsty Soul*, *Intimate Issues*, and *Intimacy Ignited*, coauthored with Lorraine Pintus.

She and her husband now live in Monument, Colorado. They have four grown children and are grandparents.